A SUPER STEELERS JOURNEY

THE 23-YEAR QUEST TO HONOR PITTSBURGH'S DYNASTY LEGENDS

MERRILL SHAFFER

SUNBURY PRESS
Mechanicsburg, PA USA

Published by Sunbury Press, Inc.
Mechanicsburg, Pennsylvania

www.sunburypress.com

ISBN: 978-1-62006-381-1 (Trade paperback)

Library of Congress Control Number: 2018954286

FIRST SUNBURY PRESS EDITION: August 2018

Product of the United States of America
0 1 1 2 3 5 8 13 21 34 55

Set in Bookman Old Style
Designed by Crystal Devine
Cover by Terry Kennedy
Edited by Lawrence Knorr

Continue the Enlightenment!

CONTENTS

1

THE MAKING OF A SUPER STEELERS FAN

My name is Merrill Shaffer, and I was destined to be a Pittsburgh Steelers fan. I was born in 1969, the same year as the birth of the greatest dynasty in football history. 1969 was the year that the Pittsburgh Steelers hired Chuck Noll to take the reins of their fledgling football team. Coach Noll changed the Steelers from lovable losers, with no playoff wins in the four decades prior to his arrival, into the powerhouse that would become the Team of the 1970s, and win a remarkable four Super Bowl titles in six years. 1969 was also the year that the Steelers drafted a little known defensive tackle from West Texas State by the name of Joe Greene. "Mean" Joe, as he would come to be known, would become the cornerstone of the Steel Curtain, the most dominant defense in the history of the National Football League. It is pretty incredible to think that these significant events that changed and shaped the course of the Pittsburgh Steelers franchise occurred at the same time that I entered the world.

However, my foray into football fandom did not start with my beloved Steelers. At a very young age, I was a different kind of fan; maybe a little too rational. I was born in New York in 1969. The Jets were the Super Bowl champions in 1969, and for that very reason, my earliest football memories revolved around Broadway Joe Namath and the Green and White. I remember proudly taking my New York Jets bubble gum machine helmet to kindergarten for show and tell, and requesting the plastic Jets helmet for my ice cream sundae at Dairy Queen (remember those!). They were prominently displayed in my bedroom. Being the hero of Super Bowl III, with his colorful personality and jet-setting style, Joe Namath was an easy choice as my first favorite player. I am also certain that a large part of the decision was based on the fact that he had appeared in an episode of *The Brady Bunch*. As a kid in the 1970s, it didn't get any cooler than that. Unfortunately, by the time I was old enough to pick the Jets as my favorite team, Broadway Joe was admittedly past his prime. I remember I "guaranteed" my father that the Jets would beat the Miami Dolphins during a game in 1974. They did not, and I cried my eyes out when they lost 21-17. Perhaps it was at that point that my allegiance began to change.

To be truthful, I was a citizen of the State of New York for only a few weeks. My father was a member of the United States Navy and I arrived a few weeks prior to his transfer to South Carolina. From there, following the birth of my brother, Jason, we moved to California. My parents were natives of Central Pennsylvania, and upon my father's honorable discharge from the Navy, we returned home to the Keystone State. We arrived at my grandparents' home in Danville, Pennsylvania on Christmas Day in 1973. As we entered 1974, it seemed as though fate was pushing me in the Steelers' direction. My first year as a permanent citizen of Pennsylvania, the Pittsburgh Steelers embarked on a remarkable season that would culminate in their victory over the Minnesota Vikings in Super Bowl IX, which started the team's Dynasty of the 70s. Another major event in my life seemed to coincide with a significant moment in Pittsburgh Steelers history.

By the time I reached elementary school, my support of the Jets began to wane. All of a sudden, these superstars in Black and Gold began to peak my interest. They were winning Super Bowls and creating some of the most memorable moments in football history. They had a cast of characters that left a starry-eyed kid in awe of their greatness. Being the odd, strangely rational young fan that I was, I now lived in Pennsylvania. What better reason could I have to change my allegiance? After the Steelers defeated the Dallas Cowboys in Super Bowl X, I was all in.

When I say that I was all in, I mean I was all in! The Jets helmets went in the dresser drawer. The Benji poster (I can't believe that I actually had a Benji poster) came down, and the Terry Bradshaw poster was taped to my bedroom door. As the decade went by, the Steelers defeated the Cowboys again in Super Bowl XIII and the Los Angeles Rams in Super Bowl XIV. My passion for the team grew. I would page through the Sears catalog, marking all of the Steelers items, with the hope that Santa Claus might bring some Black and Gold in his sack. My parents knew how much the Steelers meant to me. Although they didn't have much money at the time, my Christmases and birthdays were filled with Super Steelers memories. When I went outside in the winter, I looked like a Pittsburgh bumblebee. I had the Steelers' varsity jacket, with the gold vinyl sleeves. Man, why can't they bring those back! I would wear one today. But it didn't stop there. I had the Steelers beanie hat, Steelers gloves, Steelers mittens, Steelers belt buckle, Steelers shirts, Steelers socks, the full-size Rawlings Steelers football helmet, Steelers Action Teammate doll, Steelers posters, Steelers bubblegum helmets, Steelers buttons, Steelers pennants, Steelers pajamas, Steelers bed sheets, Tudar Steelers electric football set; you name it, I had it. My parents bought my brother and I packs upon packs of Topps football cards. Again, not being your normal young Steelers fan, I strapped my Steelers cards with rubber bands, but they had to be in a specific order; offensive starters first, followed by the backups, then the defensive starters and reserves. We had shoeboxes full of them. God bless my parents. Looking back, it is funny to see how they fueled my obsession, but they sacrificed a lot to make my childhood filled with fantastic memories.

As I moved into my teens, and then early adulthood, my passion for Steelers football never ceased. Even as the dynasty players of the 1970s began to retire and leave the team, I still revered them. As the team struggled to replace their superstar players and suffered through some lean seasons in the late 1980s and early 90s, I was still a diehard fan. When Chuck Noll handed the reins to Bill Cowher, I was thrilled when the Steelers returned as an NFL power. Although I was heartbroken when they lost Super Bowl XXX to the hated Cowboys, it was a wonderful new era for the team. Once again, their return to dominance coincided with more significant events in my life. I met my wife, Karen Travitz, in 1992, which was the 60th season of Pittsburgh Steelers football, and the first in the tenure of Coach Cowher. Karen and I were married in 1995, which happened to be the year that the Steelers won the AFC Championship and advanced to the Super Bowl for the first time since the glory years of the 1970s. Karen would come to share my love of the Black and Gold, and it has made it all the sweeter to share in the Steelers' success with her.

As the new century began, it was so satisfying to watch the Steelers' return to glory. How thrilled was Steeler Nation to see Bill Cowher finally hand another Vince Lombardi Trophy to the Rooney

Family after winning Super Bowl XL? As Santonio Holmes made his remarkable fingertip, toe-tapping catch in the corner of the end zone in the final minutes of Super Bowl XLIII, Mike Tomlin became the youngest head coach to lead his team to a championship and gave the Pittsburgh Steelers their record sixth title. These championship teams gave us a whole new set of heroes to cheer for Big Ben, The Bus, The Jaw, The Tasmanian Devil, Deebo, Da Beard, and on and on. The 2000s Steelers did seem to have glaring similarities to the Dynasty Teams of the 1970s. The Blitzburgh Defense dominated opposing teams in a similar fashion as the Steel Curtain. Big Ben played great in big games, just like the Blond Bomber. The Bus ran like Franco. Hines made incredible plays like Swann and Stallworth. It was truly a wonderful return to greatness.

I am as big of a Steelers fan today as I have ever been. As each generation of Steelers' players has come, I rejoice and celebrate the successes, and suffer and anguish with each defeat. I still collect and have more memorabilia than I could ever display. As much as I love the current Steelers teams, and those who have played before them, there will always be a special place in my heart for those magical teams from my childhood. To this day, when somebody mentions the Pittsburgh Steelers, the players from the 1970s are who I immediately think about. I still love to reminisce about their accomplishments with anyone who will listen. I watch every NFL Films segment, documentary, tribute and compilation about the 1970s Steelers teams and players on television and online. I have shelves full of books about those magnificent players and teams. I know that my childhood was not perfect, but on the biggest stage, when the lights were the brightest, those teams were perfect, and this biggest little fan was watching with wide eyes. When I think about that time in my life, I can't help but smile, and the Steelers are a big reason why. Those moments in time from my childhood were perfect. Even now, when the stressors of life seem to be conspiring against me, the Steel Curtain can still brighten my day. I can never thank them enough for the joy that they have brought to me and my family. I always felt that I wanted to do something special to honor and commemorate the greatest team that ever played the game.

It all started innocently enough. Jack Ham was making an autograph appearance at a local shopping mall in 1994. I thought it would be neat to have a Pittsburgh Steelers football helmet signed by one of the all-time greats, and one of my heroes from the Steel Curtain. Karen shared in my enjoyment of collecting Steelers memorabilia, so she was on board and we set out to purchase a helmet for the signing. To our surprise, finding a Steelers helmet in the Harrisburg, Pennsylvania area at that time was no easy task. The team's mid-1990s resurgence had apparently put Steelers helmets in short supply. After searching numerous sporting goods stores and memorabilia shops, we had struck out. Everyone told us that there had been a spike in demand and helmets were on back order. Most merchants said that they would not have any helmets prior to the date of Jack Ham's signing, and there was no indication when they would have any back in stock. Undeterred, after making dozens of telephone calls, I was finally able to find a store that was taking orders, and hoped to have Steelers helmets in stock within a few weeks. Of all places, it was a bar and game room supply store. The week prior to Jack Ham's appearance, I received a phone call stating that the store had received their shipment from Riddell, and they had our Steelers helmet. Karen drove to the store that afternoon. When she arrived, there was a pile of helmets at the back of the store, and they were all accounted for. Each of them had a tag with a customer's name, waiting to be claimed. Thank God we had reserved one. If not, our Super Steelers helmet would have never happened. Karen gave the clerk her information, and they handed her a Riddell box with a shiny new Steelers helmet inside. We were in business.

I cannot explain why we decided to try to find and obtain the signatures of the 22 players, and Coach Chuck Noll, who were members of all four of the Pittsburgh Steelers' Super Bowl Championship teams in the 1970s. I don't specifically remember how or when that decision was made. To be truthful, when we decided to start this project, I could not remember which players were actually members of all four championship teams. So, I wrote to the Pittsburgh Steelers and asked them. This was prior to the internet being readily available at the click of a button, so snail mail was our only viable option. A few weeks later, we received an envelope in the mail with the Steelers' logo, and we hastily opened it. The team was kind enough to send us copies of the rosters for each of the four Super Bowl teams. What was also neat was the sheets included the dates, times and locations of each Super Bowl game and the rosters for the opposing teams. We have always been thankful for the Steelers' wonderful response and assistance with our project, and we have saved that envelope with those rosters as special mementos from the team.

The adventure that started with Jack Ham in 1994, and culminated with Loren Toews' signature in the summer of 2017, would take Karen and me, and our family and friends on a 23-year journey. A journey filled with memories, laughter, tears, and joy to last a lifetime. What follows is the history of the men who signed our helmet and the stories of our quest to honor the Super Steelers.

2

JACK HAM

Jack Ham was born in Johnstown, Pennsylvania on December 23, 1948. He attended Bishop McCort High School, where he was a member of the football and track teams. He was an All-State linebacker his senior year. After graduating from Bishop McCort in 1966, Ham attended prep school at Massanutten Military Academy in Virginia. Amazingly, Jack Ham was not heavily recruited out of high school and was actually the last player to be offered a scholarship to Penn State University in 1967. However, Ham's talents would soon shine through, and he would develop into one of the greatest players in Nittany Lion history. He was a defensive standout during his collegiate career, helping Penn State to back to back undefeated seasons in 1968 and 1969. A co-captain and consensus All-American his senior season in 1970, Ham starred in the East/West Shrine Game, and the Hula Bowl, where he was named Outstanding Defensive Player. Jack Ham was elected to the College Football Hall of Fame in 1990. He received the Penn State University Hometown Hall of Fame honor in 2017.

In my opinion, Jack Ham is the greatest outside linebacker in NFL history. I admit that I am a bit biased in my assessment, as Ham was one of my favorite players from the 1970s Steelers, and I consider myself fortunate to have watched him play the game. He may not have been as flashy and flamboyant as others like Lawrence Taylor, Kevin Greene, Terrell Suggs or Derrick Thomas, but Jack Ham was the complete package. He was simply a model of consistency. He was equally effective when defending the pass or the run, and I would argue that he was as technically sound of a player as anyone who ever put on the pads. He didn't always wow the crowd with devastating hits, but he put opposing players on the ground, which is the job of a defender, and he never seemed out of position. His tackling technique was textbook perfect; hit with the shoulder, wrap the arms and take the runner to the ground. Ham had an incredible ability to diagnose offensive plays and gained a well-deserved reputation as a big-play defender. He was a major contributor to the Steel Curtain and made it nearly impossible to run or throw short distance passes to the left side of the defense. His play during the 1970s Super Bowls was deserving of his selection to the NFL Silver and Golden Anniversary Super Bowl Teams.

Ham was drafted by the Steelers in the second round of the 1971 NFL Draft. He played 12 seasons with the Steelers, winning four Super Bowl rings. He had a remarkable 32 interceptions as a linebacker, which is the exact same career total as former Steelers' safety Troy Polamalu. He recorded 25 ½ sacks, recovered 21 fumbles and scored two career touchdowns. His 53 career takeaways are the most in NFL history by a non-defensive back. Ham was selected to eight Pro Bowls, was a First Team All-Pro six times, named the NFL Defensive Player of the Year in 1975 by the Football Writers of America, a member of the NFL 75th Anniversary All-Time Team, selected to the NFL 1970s All-Decade Team, named to the Steelers' 50th Anniversary Team in 1982, selected to the Steelers' All-time Team in 2007 and a member of the inaugural class of the Pittsburgh Steelers' Hall of Honor in 2017. Ham was elected to the Pro Football Hall of Fame in 1988, his first year of eligibility. Jack Ham was the perfect player to start our Super Steelers helmet.

Karen and I were extremely excited when we found out that Jack Ham was scheduled to make an autograph appearance at the Camp Hill Mall in Camp Hill, Pennsylvania in the summer of 1994. After securing a hard to find Pittsburgh Steelers helmet the week prior to the signing, we took our brand-new Riddell box to the center court area of the mall and waited for Jack's arrival. The signing was scheduled to begin at 1:00 pm. However, we stood in line for close to an hour past the scheduled start time, and there was no sign of #59. All of a sudden, a bearded man came sprinting out of the Montgomery Ward store at the north end of the mall to cheers from the fans who had gathered. Sure enough, it was Jack Ham! He ran to the center of the mall and hurdled the velvet rope surrounding the gazebo where he was to conduct the signing like Edwin Moses in the Olympics. We were standing near the front of the line and, out of breath, we heard Jack tell the promoter of the signing that he had driven to the wrong mall. When Karen and I reached the front of the line, it was truly an honor to meet such a legend. Jack Ham was the first Pittsburgh Steeler I had actually met in person. We were able to talk with him for a few moments, and he then added the first signature to our helmet. Jack handed the helmet back to us with a smile and a handshake, and he wished us well. As we stopped at a nearby bench, we had the chance to observe our first Steelers autograph. Although he had the smallest name of any of the eventual signers, he, by far, has the largest signature. He signed a very large, bold autograph and added his #59. At the time, we're proud to have a beautiful Jack Ham signed Steelers helmet. Little did we know that this was the beginning of what would become our Super Steelers journey?

3

JACK LAMBERT

Jack Lambert was born in Mantua, Ohio on July 8, 1952. He attended Crestwood High School, where he starred in baseball, basketball, and football. It was at Crestwood where Lambert got his legendary toothless snarl, however, it did not come on the football field. He lost his front teeth after colliding with a teammate while playing high school basketball. At Crestwood, Lambert was an All-Conference cornerback and, ironically, played quarterback. His disdain for quarterbacks would become well known, as later in his professional career he would state that they should all wear dresses. After his freshman year, Lambert approached his coach and asked to change his number to 00. He was told that if he wanted to wear a special number, he would have to be a special player. Lambert was issued the number after his sophomore season, and was such a special player, #00 is now retired at Crestwood, and the school's football stadium was renamed in his honor.

Lambert was initially recruited as a defensive end at Kent State University. He switched positions to middle linebacker as a sophomore, and a legend was unleashed. His college biography stated that Lambert had a "lust for contact", which perfectly described his football mentality and playing style. During his collegiate career, Lambert was a two time All Mid-American Conference linebacker, 1972 MAC Defensive Player of the Year and MVP of the 1972 Tangerine Bowl. His #99 was retired at Kent State.

Jack Lambert is my all-time favorite football player. I had a subscription to *Sports Illustrated* magazine when I was a kid. Is there anyone who doesn't remember Jack Lambert's Count Dracula cover from 1984? I tore the cover off the magazine and had it hanging on my bedroom door until the day I moved out of my parent's home. I now have an autographed 16x20 image of that cover photo that Karen matted and framed. My only regret is that she won't let me hang it over our bed! Lambert was *the* man at the manliest position in all of sports; middle linebacker. I know that there have been the Nitschke's, Butkus' and Huff's before him, and the Lewis', Singletary's and Urlacher's who came afterward. However, in my book, none of them compare to the great Jack Lambert.

As a young boy, I was mesmerized by this rough, tough, toothless bundle of energy, who seemed to make every tackle. Lambert just had the look. Is there a better image that personifies Pittsburgh Steelers football than the snarl of Jack Lambert? The first time I saw him play, I was hooked. Who doesn't remember Sheriff Jack handing out some frontier justice by throwing Cliff Harris of the Dallas Cowboys to the ground in Super Bowl X after he taunted Roy Gerela for missing a field goal? Lambert was the ultimate enforcer. He perennially led the Steelers in tackles. But beyond the rough and tumble image, there was an intelligent, technically sound player, who was arguably the most versatile middle linebacker in history. Lambert was equally devastating against the run or the pass, and his unique abilities revolutionized the position. His athleticism enabled Lambert to effectively close holes in the defensive line on run plays, but also drop into pass coverage, covering the middle zone of the defensive secondary. Lambert had many memorable moments in his legendary career, however, none bigger than his interception of Los Angeles Rams' quarterback Vince Ferragamo in the closing minutes to help preserve the Steelers' victory in Super Bowl XIV. If Joe Greene was the cornerstone, Jack Lambert was the heart and soul of the Steel Curtain Defense.

Lambert was drafted in the second round of the Steelers' legendary 1974 NFL Draft class. He played 11 seasons in Pittsburgh, winning four Super Bowl championships during his career. He had 28 career interceptions and recovered 17 opponents' fumbles. Lambert was a nine-time Pro Bowl selection and named a First Team All-Pro on seven occasions. He was selected as the NFL Defensive Rookie of the Year in 1974, named NFL Defensive Player of the Year in 1976, a member of the NFL 75th Anniversary All-Time Team, selected to the NFL 1970s All-Decade Team, named to the NFL 1980s All-Decade Team, a member of the NFL Silver Anniversary Super Bowl Team, elected to the NFL Golden Anniversary Super Bowl Team, named to the Steelers' 50th Anniversary Team in 1982, selected to the Steelers' All-time Team in 2007 and a member of the inaugural class of the Pittsburgh Steelers' Hall of Honor in 2017. Jack

Lambert was inducted into the Pro Football Hall of Fame in his first year of eligibility in 1990.

Jack Lambert made an autograph appearance at the Camp Hill Mall on June 17, 1995. I have to admit, I was really excited, and really nervous, to meet my all-time football hero. I could hardly contain myself when Karen and I got to the mall with our helmet. There was already a large crowd of Steelers fans awaiting Jack's arrival. Suddenly, we heard the crowd start to cheer. We turned, and there was Jack Lambert walking towards us. As he walked towards the center of the mall, the crowd began chanting his name, but Jack seemed almost embarrassed by the outpouring of adulation. He waved to the fans as he reached the autograph table and said, "Ok, let's get this started!" As we neared the front of the line, I was overcome with excitement to meet Jack Lambert. All the memories of his wonderful career flooded my memory. When we got to the table and we were face to face with Jack, I don't think I could speak. He greeted us with a hello and we handed him our helmet. Jack took it and said, "I'll put it right next to my buddy, Hammy." He placed his signature and #58 alongside Jack Ham's autograph, we shook hands and Jack wished us well. I walked away, still in awe of the man I had worshiped as a child. At that point in time, even if we weren't able to complete our helmet, we were thrilled to add the autograph of my all-time favorite Steeler.

4

FRANCO HARRIS

Franco Harris was born on March 7, 1950, in Fort Dix, New Jersey. He attended Rancocas Valley Regional High School. At Rancocas Valley, Harris played baseball, basketball, and football. He was a high school All-American running back and received the Rancocas Valley Regional High School Hometown Hall of Fame honor in 2012. He earned a football scholarship as a fullback to Penn State University in 1968. Ironically, Harris was often overshadowed by and used as a blocking back for teammate Lydell Mitchell during his career with the Nittany Lions. Still, Harris finished his collegiate career with 2,002 rushing yards and scored 24 touchdowns. Although Lydell Mitchell was generally considered to be the better NFL prospect, the Pittsburgh Steelers were so impressed by Harris' rushing and pass catching abilities and potential, they drafted him 35 picks ahead of Mitchell, who was ultimately selected by the Baltimore Colts and played against his former teammate throughout the 1970s.

It is no coincidence that the Pittsburgh Steelers won their very first playoff game in Franco Harris's rookie season. Who could ever forget how the Steelers won that game? On December 23, 1972, the Steelers faced off against the Oakland Raiders in an epic defensive battle in the AFC divisional playoff game at Three Rivers Stadium in Pittsburgh. Trailing 7-6 with 22 seconds remaining, the Steelers faced 4th and 10 on their own 40-yard line. Quarterback Terry Bradshaw rolled out of the pocket and fired a pass to the Raiders' 35-yard line. Raiders' safety Jack Tatum collided with Steelers' running back John "Frenchy" Fuqua, and the ball flew backward, seemingly ending the Steelers' season. Out of nowhere, Franco Harris scooped up the ball before it hit the turf and raced into the end zone, giving the Steelers a miraculous victory, and their first-ever postseason win. Of course, that famous play is now known as "The Immaculate Reception", and it was the start of one of the greatest dynasties in sports history.

Before Franco Harris arrived in Pittsburgh, the Steelers were putting together the pieces of a championship caliber team. After he arrived, they became champions. Harris provided a spectacular and devastating running game that enabled the Steelers to become a Super Bowl contender. Franco Harris' importance to the Steelers' dynasty cannot be overstated. A perennial Pro Bowler, Harris was a consistent 1,000-yard rusher, who played brilliantly in big games. He was the MVP of Super Bowl IX, torching the Minnesota Vikings for a then-Super Bowl record 158 yards rushing. When he retired, Harris ranked third in NFL history in career rushing yards.

Franco Harris was drafted as a halfback in the first round of the 1972 NFL Draft. He played 12 seasons in Pittsburgh, winning four Super Bowl championships. Harris ended his career with 12,120 rushing yards and 91 touchdowns, averaging 4.1 yards per carry. He also contributed 307 career receptions and scored 9 receiving touchdowns. Harris added 354 rushing yards and scored 4 touchdowns in the Steelers' four Super Bowl Championships in the 1970s. He was named to nine Pro Bowls, was a First Team All-Pro in 1977, was voted the NFL Offensive Rookie of the Year in 1972, named to the NFL 1970s All-Decade Team, a member of the NFL Silver Anniversary Super Bowl Team, selected to the NFL Golden Anniversary Super Bowl Team, elected to the Steelers' 50th Anniversary Team in 1982, selected to the Steelers' All-time Team in 2007 and a member of the inaugural class of the Pittsburgh Steelers' Hall of Honor in 2017. Franco Harris was honored as the NFL Man of the Year award in 1976. Harris was elected to the Pennsylvania Sports Hall of Fame in 2008. He was inducted into the Pro Football Hall of Fame in 1990, his first year of eligibility. Of all his on-field honors, Harris is perhaps best remembered by the Steelers' fans as the leader of Franco's Italian Army, who even counted Frank Sinatra as a member of their ranks.

In 1995, I worked for a wholesale food distributor in Harrisburg, Pennsylvania. In June of that year, the company was planning to hold a food show for their customers at the Pennsylvania State Farm Show Complex. It was decided that the show would have a sports theme, and the company brought in several retired athletes to mingle with customers and sign autographs. After his retirement from the NFL, Franco Harris started a company that made nutrition-oriented foods for school children with his former Penn State teammate, Lydell Mitchell. Our company carried Franco's line of products, and he was one of the former athletes scheduled to appear at the food show.

The owner of the brokerage firm that sold Franco's products to our company was named Michael Bell. Over the years, I had become quite acquainted with Mike, and he was well aware of the Steelers helmet we had started the previous year. To my disappointment, I was not picked to be a member of the work crew that would be at the food show. Mike approached me a week prior to the opening of the show and said that he was bringing Franco, and I should have our helmet ready. When I told him that I would not be attending the food show, he paused for a moment. Mike didn't miss a beat and told me to have our helmet at work with me the following Thursday, the last day of the show.

I did as Mike had instructed and had our helmet in a locker at work on the last day of the food show. I was standing on the dock of our warehouse when all of a sudden, Franco Harris walked through the door. Mike followed Franco in the door and he told me to grab our helmet. I ran to my locker and retrieved the helmet and a paint marker. Franco took the helmet, looked at the other signatures and commented about how nice our helmet looked. He placed a big, bold autograph on the back of the helmet, at the top, near the stripe. Franco gave me a firm handshake and cautioned me to allow enough time for the paint to dry. I thanked Franco and looked over at Mike, who was leaning against with wall, with a sly grin on his face. As I thanked him for making this wonderful moment possible, Mike gave me a quick wink.

Little did I know what had taken place prior to Franco's arrival. Mike had indeed taken Franco to the food show earlier that day. Apparently, Franco had walked the show floor and mingled with customers prior to sitting at a table to sign autographs. He had a steady line of autograph seekers until the early afternoon. All of a sudden, Mike interrupted the autograph session and stated that Franco had to catch a plane. Franco was abruptly escorted to Mike's awaiting car, leaving a long line of confused and angry customers. Now Franco may very well have had a plane to catch, but I am certain that Mike took Franco from the food show so that he could keep his promise to have him sign our helmet. After I found out what Mike had done, it made his little smile and wink that much more special and meaningful. Sadly, Mike has since passed away, but we will always have fond memories of him and that special day with Franco Harris. He played a huge role in helping us complete our Super Steelers helmet and its people like Mike that made this such a wonderful journey.

5

MEL BLOUNT

Mel Blount was born in Vidalia, Georgia on April 10, 1948. He excelled at baseball, basketball, football, and track at Lyons Industrial High School. Blount received the Lyons Industrial High School Hometown Hall of Fame honor in 2012. He earned a football scholarship to Southern University in 1966, where he played cornerback and safety. Blount was a collegiate standout at Southern, being named the Southwestern Athletic Conference Most Valuable Player as a junior, and twice was selected to the SWAC All-Conference Team. He was voted team MVP as a junior and senior and was selected as a Pro-Scouts All-American at both safety and cornerback. Blount was inducted into the Louisiana Sports Hall of Fame in 1989, the Georgia Sports Hall of Fame in 1990 and the Pennsylvania Sports Hall of Fame in 2012.

Blount was the most dominant cornerback in NFL history. This fact was solidified in 1978, when the league imposed rules changes to prevent defensive backs from contacting receivers beyond five yards from the line of scrimmage, in an attempt to open up the passing game. This became known as "The Mel Blount Rule". It forever changed the way the game is played and showed just how dominant Blount was for the Steel Curtain Defense. Blount absolutely overwhelmed receivers, and the changes to the rules had little effect on his success, as he was elected to three Pro Bowls after the changes were made. He was the epitome of a shutdown cornerback. Blount became a starter for the Steelers in 1972, and he did not allow a single touchdown pass against him that season. He intercepted at least one pass in each of his 14 seasons with the Steelers and led the NFL with 11 takeaways in 1975. He ended his career with a club record 57 interceptions. Blount also recovered 13 opponents' fumbles. He scored two career touchdowns. Mel Blount was an integral member of the Steelers' Dynasty of the 70s, and his play was superb in their four Super Bowl wins. He had a key interception of Fran Tarkington at the goal line near the end of the first half of Super Bowl IX against the Minnesota Vikings. His timely interception of Roger Staubach of the Dallas Cowboys in Super Bowl XIII started the drive that resulted in the Steelers' go-ahead touchdown.

The Pittsburgh Steelers selected Mel Blount in the third round of the NFL Draft in 1970. He played 14 seasons in the Black and Gold, winning four Super Bowl rings. He was selected to five Pro Bowls, voted MVP of the Pro Bowl Game in 1976, a First Team All-Pro on four occasions, voted the 1975 NFL Defensive Player of the Year by the Associated Press, named to the NFL 1980s All-Decade Team, a member of the NFL Silver Anniversary Super Bowl Team, selected to the NFL Golden Anniversary Super Bowl Team, elected to the Steelers' 50th Anniversary Team in 1982, selected to the Steelers' All-time Team in 2007 and a member of the inaugural class of the Pittsburgh Steelers' Hall of Honor in 2017. Mel Blount was inducted into the Pro Football Hall of Fame in his first year of eligibility in 1989.

Karen and I were extremely excited when we learned that Mel Blount would be taking part in an autograph signing at the Colonial Park Mall in Harrisburg, Pennsylvania on July 15, 1995. It was a great opportunity to add another dynasty legend to our Super Steelers helmet. When Mel Blount arrived for the signing, he was wearing his familiar cowboy hat and waved to the large crowd that had gathered as he walked to the autograph area. We marveled at how great he looked. Mel looked as though he could have suited up in his Black and Gold #47 uniform and played man to man coverage against Jerry Rice that afternoon! When we arrived at the autograph table, Mel was very friendly and soft-spoken. He greeted us with a smile and a hello, and we handed him our helmet. Before we had the chance to offer him our paint marker, which we had used for each previous signature, Mel had signed the helmet on the back, using a marker that the promoter had provided him. The ink was much thicker than the other signatures already on our helmet, but Mel's autograph looked terrific. He shook our hands and wished us well. As we walked away from the autograph area, we admired Mel's signature and were happy and honored to have added another member of the Steel Curtain to our helmet.

6

JOE GREENE

Charles Edward Greene, better known as Joe Greene, was born on September 24, 1946, in Temple, Texas. He got his nickname, "Joe" (nicknamed after heavyweight boxing champion Joe Louis), from his aunt. He got his other, more famous nickname, "Mean Joe", for his dominance on the football field. Greene attended Dunbar High School where he played football, basketball and was a member of the track team. Despite his excellent play, Greene was not heavily recruited and received few scholarship offers after his scholastic career. He eventually accepted a football scholarship from North Texas State University (now the University of North Texas) in 1964. At North Texas State, Greene was a three-time All-Missouri Valley Conference selection and a consensus All-American defensive tackle as a senior in 1968. He was the leader of a defense that was so dominant that in his 29 games played for North Texas State, opponents averaged less than two yards per rushing attempt. Although they were known as the Eagles during his playing career, the University of North Texas is now known as the Mean Green, in no small part to Joe Greene's spectacular collegiate career. His #75 was retired and he was inducted into the University of North Texas Hall of Fame in 1981. Joe Greene was elected to the College Football Hall of Fame in 1984. He received the Dunbar High School Hometown Hall of Fame honor and was awarded the Distinguished Alumni Award from Temple Independent School District in 2015. Greene was elected to the Texas High School Football Hall of Fame in 2017.

The Pittsburgh Steelers franchise changed forever on January 28, 1969. On that date, the Steelers selected defensive lineman Joe Greene from North Texas State with the fourth pick in the NFL Draft. Greene would become the cornerstone of the Dynasty of the 1970s, and he is widely considered to be the greatest Pittsburgh

Steelers player of all-time. However, his selection was initially viewed with skepticism amongst the fans and media in Pittsburgh, with the headline in one of the local newspapers reading, "Who's Joe Greene?" upon being drafted by the Steelers. It did not take long for Pittsburgh and the football world to know "Mean" Joe Greene.

Prior to the arrival of Joe Greene, the Steelers had never won a playoff game, and they were viewed as lovable losers. That changed forever when Greene donned the Black and Gold. He changed the culture of the organization and showed that losing was not acceptable. There, perhaps, has never been a more devastating defensive player in the history of the league. Greene was virtually unblockable and single handily dominated games. He developed the Stunt 4-3 Defense, in which he would line up at an angle between the center and guard. This often resulted in Greene being double or triple teamed by opposing blockers, but it allowed other defenders to wreak havoc in opposing backfields. Greene teamed with L.C. Greenwood, Ernie Holmes, and Dwight White to form the legendary Steel Curtain, one of the most dominant defensive lines in NFL history. The unit was even featured on the cover of *Time* magazine. Greene played great in the biggest games and was a major contributor to each of Pittsburgh's four Super Bowl championships in the 1970s. He is remembered by Steelers fans for recording an interception, forced fumble and fumble recovery in the team's victory over the Minnesota Vikings in Super Bowl IX. He was credited with 78 ½ sacks and recovered 16 opponents' fumbles in his brilliant 13-year career with the Steelers.

Joe Greene's accomplishments are staggering. He was a four-time Super Bowl Champion, ten-time Pro Bowl selection, six-time First Team All-Pro, voted NFL Defensive Player of the Year by the Associated Press in 1972 and 1974, named NFL Defensive Rookie of the Year in 1969, named NFL Man of the Year in 1979, a member of the NFL 75th Anniversary All-Time Team, selected to the NFL 1970s All-Decade Team, named to the NFL Silver Anniversary Super Bowl Team, a member of the NFL Golden Anniversary Super Bowl Team, elected to the Steelers' 50th Anniversary Team in 1982, selected to the Steelers' All-Time Team in 2007 and a member of the inaugural class of the Pittsburgh Steelers' Hall of Honor in 2017. Joe Greene's #75 was officially retired by the Steelers in 2014, becoming only the second player in the team's history to be so honored. Greene was elected to the Pro Football Hall of Fame in 1987 in his first year of eligibility.

Joe Greene's accomplishments on the football field made him a legend. However, it was off the field that he provided me, and millions of other fans, with one of my fondest childhood memories. Who could ever forget "Mean" Joe's now iconic Coca-Cola commercial in 1979? It is perhaps the greatest commercial in television history, and I could not help being jealous of the little boy having Joe Greene toss him his game jersey. It was annually voted the greatest Super Bowl commercial of all-time, and Greene won a Clio award in 1980 for advertising excellence. Whether it's on the gridiron or Madison Avenue, "Mean" Joe Greene is a true champion.

Karen and I were ecstatic when we learned that Joe Greene would be making an autograph appearance at the East Mall in Harrisburg, Pennsylvania in the summer of 1995. However, I had to work that particular Saturday, so for the first time, Karen would be flying solo for an autograph event. She was anxious and nervous about carrying our helmet into the mall, and she wrapped it in a blanket to try to conceal it from any would-be thieves. When Mr. Greene arrived for the signing, there did not appear to be anyone running the event. After waiting several minutes, Joe simply sat down at the autograph table and began signing on his own. As Karen approached the table, she was unsure what to do, as she only had a plain red ticket and no one appeared to be taking them. She finally stood face to face with "Mean" Joe and she dropped the ticket on the table next to him. Joe took our helmet and added a big, bold signature on the front next to the Steelers' logo. As Joe handed the helmet back to Karen, she stood there with a confused look on her face. At previous signings, we had usually received our ticket back, showing the date and location of the event, and providing some form of authenticity. However, that was not the case this time. Being a rookie of how the process worked, Karen decided to ask "Mean" Joe, himself, if he was going to provide the authenticity. I wish I could have witnessed this interaction because Joe apparently didn't respond well to Karen's question. He said, "Authenticity? I'll give you authenticity! I'll bop you in the head!" At that point, Karen thought it would be wise to avoid the sack and got the heck out of there! I arrived at the mall a short time later, and Karen recalled her encounter with "Mean" Joe. I couldn't help but laugh, knowing that Joe was joking with her, but she made it clear that she was never going solo for another signing again. Years later, Karen now loves to tell the story of how she risked bodily harm at the hands of “Mean” Joe Greene, for the sake of completing our helmet. In truth, Karen enjoyed her “encounter” with Joe, and we are truly honored to have the signature of the greatest Steeler of all-time on our helmet.

7

ROCKY BLEIER

The story of Rocky Bleier is the stuff of legends. His athletic accomplishments included a National Championship at the University of Notre Dame, and a tremendously successful NFL career, winning four Super Bowl championships with the Pittsburgh Steelers. But none of these achievements can compare to the honorable service he gave to our country during the Vietnam War. His life and military service have been well documented, with a bestselling biography and a made for television movie starring Robert Urich. Rocky Bleier is truly an American hero.

Robert Patrick Bleier was born in Appleton, Wisconsin on March 5, 1946. He was given his famous nickname as a baby. Living above the family's tavern, his father would bring customers to see his newborn son, who he said looked like a little rock in his crib. The moniker stuck, and little Robert would be forever known as Rocky. Bleier attended Xavier High School where he starred on the football, basketball and track teams. He was a three-time All-State running back, and an All-Conference linebacker and defensive back. The football stadium at Xavier was renamed Rocky Bleier Field in his honor, and his #23 has been retired. A street in his hometown of Appleton was renamed Rocky Bleier Run in 2007. Bleier earned a football scholarship to the University of Notre Dame in 1964. He helped lead the Fighting Irish to the 1966 National Championship as a junior. He was named team captain as a senior. Bleier was selected by the Pittsburgh Steelers in the 16th round of the 1968 NFL Draft.

After being selected by the Steelers, Rocky Bleier was drafted into the United States Army in December of 1968. He served in combat in the Vietnam War and was seriously wounded by enemy rifle fire and a grenade explosion during an ambush in Heip Duc on August 20, 1969. Bleier suffered debilitating injuries to his feet and legs and spent six weeks in a medical hospital in Tokyo, Japan. He was classified as 40 percent disabled and was told by doctors that he would never play football again. While hospitalized, Bleier received a postcard from Steelers owner Art Rooney, telling him that the team wasn't playing well and they needed him to return. Remarkably, Bleier rejoined the Steelers in 1970. He went through several years of agonizing surgeries and rehabilitation before finally earning a spot in the Steelers' starting backfield in 1974. He was a major contributor for Pittsburgh's dynasty teams, including a 1,000-yard rushing season in 1976. That year, he and Franco Harris became only the second backfield combination to each rush for 1,000 yards in the same season. Bleier was a starter on all four of the Steelers' Super Bowl teams in the 1970s. He will always be remembered by Steelers' fans for his fantastic leaping catch against the Dallas Cowboys just before halftime to give Pittsburgh a lead that they would never relinquish in Super Bowl XIII. That sensational play graced the cover of *Sports Illustrated.* He played 12 seasons for the Steelers. Bleier was named to the Steelers' 50th Anniversary Team in 1982 and the Steelers' All-Time Team in 2007. He was elected to the Pittsburgh Steelers' Hall of Honor in 2018. However, perhaps Rocky Bleier's most impressive honors came from his military service. He was awarded the Bronze Star Medal, Purple Heart and Combat Infantryman Badge.

Rocky Bleier was scheduled to make an autograph appearance at the Valley Forge Convention Center in Valley Forge, Pennsylvania on September 16, 1995. Karen and I were thrilled and honored to add Rocky's signature to our helmet. We were approximately halfway back in the autograph line when Rocky arrived. However, it took what seemed like an eternity to finally make our way to the front of the line. But the reason for the long wait was fantastic and well worth the time. Rocky could not have been nicer to each and every fan. When Karen and I met Rocky, he took several moments to talk with us, ask us where we were from, and to our stunned amazement, offered us a chance to view and actually hold all four of this Super Bowl rings. They were absolutely beautiful. It was the first time we had ever actually seen a real Super Bowl ring, and it was truly an honor and privilege to touch them. Rocky took our helmet and boldly signed his autograph and #20 on the back. This was truly one of the most memorable experiences in our Super Steelers journey.

Over the years, we have had the pleasure of having several memorable encounters with Rocky Bleier. He was good friends with the family that owned the Rutherford Café in Harrisburg, Pennsylvania. The family would occasionally have Rocky come to the restaurant for private parties during football seasons. We were fortunate to have been invited to spend a Sunday afternoon watching the Steelers and throw back a few Iron City's with Rocky Bleier. We had another great visit with Rocky at the Team of the Decade Reunion in Pittsburgh in 1999 and met with him after he spoke at a charity event in Lancaster, Pennsylvania several years later. Rocky Bleier will always have a special place in the hearts of not only Steeler Nation but a grateful country, as well. He is quite a remarkable man.

8

MIKE WEBSTER AND JOHN STALLWORTH

Mike Webster was born on March 18, 1952, in Tomahawk, Wisconsin. He attended Rhinelander High School where he was a state place winner in wrestling and threw shot put for the track team. However, he did not start playing football until he was a junior in high school. In just two years of varsity action, Webster excelled and caught the eye of college scouts. He earned a football scholarship to the University of Wisconsin, where he was an honor student and a three-year starter on the offensive line. He earned Second Team All-Big Ten Conference honors his junior year in 1972 and was First Team All-Big Ten Conference in 1973. He was the Badgers' team Most Valuable Player as a senior. Webster was elected to the Wisconsin Athletic Hall of Fame in 2007. The football stadium at Rhinelander High School was renamed Mike Webster Stadium in his honor.

The Pittsburgh Steelers selected Mike Webster in the fifth round of their legendary 1974 NFL Draft Class. Webster will always be known as the Steelers' Iron Man, and he is arguably the greatest center in the history of the league. He anchored an offensive line that produced perennial 1,000-yard rushers and protected the Pittsburgh aerial assault on offense. Webster was smart, strong, durable and dependable, and he played 15 seasons in Pittsburgh, more than any other player in Steelers history. At one point, he had started 150 straight games for the Steelers. He was responsible for the blocking assignments and adjustments for the Steelers' offensive line, and as Terry Bradshaw said in Webster's presentation speech during his Hall of Fame induction, he was the team's rock and they leaned on him. Webster was an invaluable member of the Steelers' dynasty teams in the 1970s. He was the last of the 22 players who won all four of the Steelers' Super Bowl Championships in the 1970s to retire from the NFL. Perhaps no other Steelers player better represented the blue-collar image of Pittsburgh.

Mike Webster was a nine-time Pro Bowl selection, seven-time First-Team All-Pro, named to the NFL's 75th Anniversary Team, the NFL 1970s All-Decade Team, the NFL 1980s All-Decade Team, voted to the NFL Silver Anniversary Super Bowl Team, a member of the NFL Golden Anniversary Super Bowl Team, named to the Steelers' 50th Anniversary Team in 1982, selected to the Steelers' All-Time Team in 2007 and a member of the inaugural class of the Pittsburgh Steelers' Hall of Honor in 2017. Mike Webster was elected to the Pro Football Hall of Fame in his first year of eligibility in 1997.

Sadly, Mike Webster passed away on September 24, 2002, at the age of 50. His death has brought much-documented attention to the issues of the neurodegenerative disease chronic traumatic encephalopathy (CTE) amongst former NFL players and athletes from other contact sports. He was the first former NFL player to be diagnosed with CTE. It was heartbreaking to see the decline in Webster's health and the unfortunate events that occurred at the end of his life, including periods of homelessness and prescription drug abuse. However, that is not how I choose to remember Mike Webster. He will always be "Iron" Mike. Even now, as tragic as it was that his life ended far too soon, his spirit has made the game safer, and he is protecting those who have come after him, just as he protected the pocket in his glory days. God bless you, Mike Webster.

John Stallworth was born in Tuscaloosa, Alabama on July 15, 1952. Initially diagnosed with polio, Stallworth was paralyzed for a period as a child. Fortunately, he overcame his illness and became a star football player at Tuscaloosa Central High School as a running back, where he was a team captain. Stallworth received the Tuscaloosa Central High School Hometown Hall of Fame honor in 2012. In 2014, he was named the greatest high school football player of all-time from Tuscaloosa by AL.com. He earned a football scholarship to Alabama A&M University in 1970. While playing at Alabama A&M, Stallworth switched positions to wide receiver and went on to break school records for single game and career receptions. He was an All-Southern Intercollegiate Athletic Conference selection in 1972 and 1973. Stallworth was invited to participate in the 1973 Senior Bowl. His number was officially retired by Alabama

A&M in 1974. Stallworth was inducted into the Black College Football Hall of Fame in 2014.

Stallworth was selected in the fourth round of the 1974 NFL Draft by the Pittsburgh Steelers. After injuries initially stalled his promising career, he would go on to become one of the greatest wide receivers in NFL history. He was a model of consistency and would team with Lynn Swann to become possibly the game's greatest receiving tandem. An incredible route runner with fantastic speed, Stallworth made every bit of spectacular plays as his receiving partner. He would end his career as the team's all-time leader in single game and career receptions, career receiving yardage and second in career touchdowns. Stallworth had 537 receptions, 8,723 receiving yards and scored 63 touchdowns. However, Stallworth played his greatest games on the biggest stage. He was spectacular in Pittsburgh's Super Bowl wins in the 1970s. He holds Super Bowl records for yards per catch for his career (24.4), and a single game (40.33 in Super Bowl XIV). He will be remembered by Steelers' fans for his terrific 28-yard touchdown catch in the corner of the end zone to open the scoring in the first quarter, and his 75-yard touchdown catch and run in the second quarter against the Dallas Cowboys in Super Bowl XIII. However, he is perhaps better remembered for his 73-yard over the shoulder catch for the go-ahead touchdown in the fourth quarter of Super Bowl XIV, which was immortalized on the cover of *Sports Illustrated*. Stallworth had receptions in 17 consecutive games in the postseason for the Steelers, and he had 12 career postseason touchdowns.

John Stallworth played in three Pro Bowls, was a First Team All-Pro in 1979, named 1984 Comeback Player of the Year by the Pro Football Writers, was named to the Steelers' 50th Anniversary Team in 1982, voted to the Steelers' All-Time Team in 2007 and a member of the inaugural class of the Pittsburgh Steelers' Hall of Honor in 2017. He was elected to the Pro Football Hall of Fame in 2002. After his retirement, John Stallworth became a minority owner of the Pittsburgh Steelers in 2009.

Karen and I were fortunate that Mike Webster and John Stallworth were making an autograph appearance at the Camp Hill Mall on October 7, 1995. Mike Webster was scheduled to begin signing at noon, and John Stallworth at 2:30 pm. When Mike arrived, he looked fantastic, and there did not appear to be any of the lingering issues that would later plague him. We were fortunate to have met him before the onset of his later health problems. He greeted us with a smile and we had the chance to briefly chat with him. He placed a bold signature and his #52 on the back of our helmet. Karen and I left the autograph area and waited for John Stallworth to arrive.

As Mike Webster finished his autograph session, John Stallworth arrived. It was truly wonderful to watch these two old teammates interact with one another. It appeared as though they had not seen each other in some time, and they shared a long, heartfelt embrace. After speaking for several minutes, Mike appeared to give John his contact information. This was such a special moment shared by two Steelers legends.

As John Stallworth made his way to the autograph area, he, too, looked as though he could have suited up and played that afternoon. John was very kind and greeted us with a handshake. He took our helmet and autographed it on the back, with his #82. The first half of the Barnum and Bailey Act in Cleats had been secured! This was a really special day that we were able to share with two old friends.

9

L.C. GREENWOOD AND DWIGHT WHITE

L.C. Greenwood was born in Canton, Mississippi on September 8, 1946. He attended Rogers High School, where he excelled in academics and did not even begin playing sports until his junior year. He played football and basketball, but due to responsibilities at home, he had to choose between the two sports. Fortunately, he chose football. Upon his graduation, Greenwood was offered a partial academic scholarship to attend Clark College in Atlanta, Georgia. However, he chose to accept a full athletic scholarship to play football at Arkansas AM&N College (now known as the University of Arkansas at Pine Bluff) in 1965. At Arkansas AM&N, Greenwood started as a freshman on the defensive line, playing both defensive end and tackle during his collegiate career. He was a standout college player and was named All-American his senior season in 1968 by *Ebony* magazine.

Greenwood was drafted by the Steelers in the tenth round of the 1969 NFL Draft. After watching his outstanding career in Pittsburgh, it is stunning that so many teams misjudged Greenwood. He would go on to become a member of the Steelers' legendary Steel Curtain defensive line. Arguably the unit's best pass rusher, Greenwood wreaked havoc on opposing offenses. He was tall and lean, with exceptional speed off the ball. His size and quickness made it nearly impossible for offensive tackles to block him in the pass rush. At 6'6", Greenwood's height enabled him to regularly bat down opponents' passes at the line of scrimmage. He was credited with 73 ½ career sacks, recovered 14 opponents' fumbles and recorded one career safety. Greenwood was a major contributor to the success of the Steelers' four Super Bowl championship teams in the 1970s. He recorded five sacks in the four Super Bowls in which he played, including four sacks of the Cowboys' quarterback Roger Staubach in Super Bowl X.

Although he is not a member of the Pro Football Hall of Fame, L.C. Greenwood's career certainly seems worthy of his induction in Canton. Greenwood was selected to six Pro Bowls, named First Team All-Pro on two occasions, a member of the NFL 1970s All-Decade Team, voted to the NFL Silver Anniversary Super Bowl Team, named to the Steelers' 50th Anniversary Team in 1982, selected to the Steelers' All-Time Team in 2007 and a member of the inaugural class of the Pittsburgh Steelers' Hall of Honor in 2017.

Aside from L.C. Greenwood's phenomenal accomplishments on the football field, he was also known for his flair for fashion. Greenwood's style off the field earned him the nickname "Hollywood Bags". He will be forever remembered for the gold shoes that he began sporting in 1973. There have been numerous reasons given for why Greenwood wore his gold cleats. One stated that he suffered an ankle injury and needed to wear high top shoes. Not liking the black cleats he was given, he requested that the Steelers' training staff paint them gold. After recovering from the injury, Greenwood stopped wearing them, and the Steelers lost a game. So, Greenwood, again, donned the gold shoes and continued wearing them out of superstition. However, Greenwood also claimed that he wore the gold shoes so that everyone would know that he was the one who had made a play, claiming that stadium announcers were constantly giving Joe Greene credit for his tackles. Whatever the reason, Greenwood's gold shoes became iconic in NFL lore.

Karen and I had the opportunity to meet Greenwood several times over the years. Once, I asked him how much he was fined for wearing the gold shoes, which were a violation of the NFL's dress code. He replied, "Come on, man. Everybody knows that." When I shook my head stating that I did not, he said, "$100 bucks a game!" There is no official information as to whether or not the fines were every actually collected by the league. Sadly, L.C. Greenwood passed away on September 29, 2013, in Pittsburgh at the age of 67.

Dwight White was born on July 30, 1949, in Hampton, Virginia. He attended James Madison High School in Dallas, Texas. White earned a football scholarship to East Texas State University (now known as Texas A&M University-Commerce). He was a two-time All-Lone Star Conference selection at defensive tackle. White was inducted into the Pennsylvania Sports Hall of Fame in 2004. He was elected to the Lone Star Conference Hall of Honor in 2011.

Following his excellent career at East Texas State, White was taken by the Pittsburgh Steelers in the fourth round of the 1971 NFL Draft. He earned the nickname "Mad Dog" due to his intensity on the field. Blessed with great strength and quickness, he was an extremely effective pass rusher, but also outstanding defending the run. White was the epitome of the Steel Curtain Defense; physical, tenacious, relentless and vicious. He won four Super Bowl championships with the Steelers in the 1970s, was selected to two Pro Bowls, named to the Steelers' 50th Anniversary Team in 1982 and voted to the Steelers' All-Time Team in 2007.

White will always be remembered for scoring the Steelers' first-ever points in a Super Bowl by downing Minnesota Vikings' quarterback Fran Tarkington in the end zone for a safety in Super Bowl IX. But the heart of Dwight White can be measured by the fact that he even played a down in Super Bowl IX. In the week leading up to the game, White was hospitalized with pneumonia and had lost 20 pounds. To the shock of his own teammates, White played the entire game and helped the Steel Curtain hold the Vikings to 119 total yards, including only 17 rushing yards, on their way to their first World Championship. White was certainly a key contributor to the Super Steelers teams of the 1970s.

We were very fortunate to meet Dwight White several times, and each was an occasion to remember. At the Team of the Decade reunion in Pittsburgh in 1999, Dwight enthusiastically greeted us in the hotel restaurant at breakfast. He shook Karen's hand like she had just sacked Roger Staubach in the Super Bowl. She later commented that Dwight's grip was so strong that he put a dent in her college class ring. At a fundraiser near our home at the Campbelltown Fire Company in 2007, Dwight got Karen again. As she posed for a picture with "Mad Dog", he put his hand, with a huge Super Bowl XIII ring on his finger, over Karen's face just as the camera flashed. I will never forget his deep belly laugh as Dwight exclaimed, "We really got her on that one!" He then took a beautiful photo with Karen that we cherish to this day. Dwight was definitely one of our favorite Steelers. We were deeply saddened when Dwight White died on June 6, 2008, in Pittsburgh at the age of 58.

The front four of the Steel Curtain was scheduled to make an autograph appearance together at the Pennsylvania State Farm Show Complex in Harrisburg on June 22, 1996. Karen was unable to attend the signing, so this time, I was going solo. There was a dilemma as I prepared to attend the autograph session. Joe Greene had already signed our helmet, and, unfortunately, Ernie Holmes was not a member of all four of the Steelers' championship teams. He had played in Super Bowls IX and X but was not with the club when they won their championships in 1978 and 1979. Prior to the signing, I did not know if I would be able to obtain autograph tickets for just L.C. Greenwood and Dwight White, or if they were being sold as a group? When I arrived for the signing, I was able to get individual tickets, however, all four players were sitting at one table. I wasn't exactly sure how I was going to handle the situation. Joe Greene was easy; he had already signed our helmet, but I really did not want to insult Ernie Holmes.

Joe Greene was the first player at the head of the autograph table. He reached out to grab our helmet and I told him that he had already signed it. He waved me on and I moved to the left. Next was L.C. Greenwood. L.C. took the helmet and placed a bold signature on the front, to the left of the Steelers' logo. I smiled and thanked him, but I didn't have time for a long interaction, as Ernie Holmes was next in line. L.C. had set the helmet on the table and slid it in front of Ernie, assuming he would be the next to sign it. As Ernie reached for a marker, I slid the helmet past him. He seemed to be scanning the signatures, and almost sounding like a child, he asked, "You got me on there?" I felt like such a heel. Completely lying, I responded, "Yeah Ernie, you're already on there." I slid to my left and was standing in front of Dwight White. Dwight was jovial and smoking a cigar at the end of the table. He picked up our helmet and added a beautiful signature on the back. I shook his hand and left the autograph area feeling like I had just committed a crime. I was really happy to have added L.C. and Dwight's autographs to our helmet, but I truly felt awful for lying to Ernie Holmes, who really seemed to want to be a part of our project. I swore that if we had the chance in the future, I would have him sign something to add to our Steelers collection. Happily, a few years later, we had each member of the Steel Curtain sign a gorgeous print of the front four, and we now have Ernie Holmes' autograph hanging on our office wall.

10

TERRY BRADSHAW

Terry Bradshaw was born on September 2, 1948, in Shreveport, Louisiana. He was a multisport star at Woodlawn High School. He set a national record in the javelin as a senior, with a throw of 243' 7". This feat earned Bradshaw a spot in *Sports Illustrated* magazine's Faces in the Crowd section. But it was on the football field where Bradshaw had his greatest moments. Highly recruited for his accurate and powerful throwing arm, he led Woodlawn to the 1965 Louisiana AAA High School Championship Game. Bradshaw received the Woodlawn High School Hometown Hall of Fame honor in 2013. He accepted a football scholarship to Louisiana Tech University in 1966. During his collegiate career, he would go on to become the nation's top quarterback prospect. Bradshaw was an All-American selection in his junior and senior seasons and held virtually every passing record at Louisiana Tech. He led the NCAA with 2,890 total yards of offense in his junior year, and his 2,314 total yards were fourth in the nation his senior season. Bradshaw finished his collegiate career with 7,149 passing yards and 42 touchdown passes. He was the Most Valuable Player of the 1969 Senior Bowl. Bradshaw was inducted into the Louisiana Tech Athletic Hall of Fame in 1984, and his #12 was retired by the school. He was voted to the Louisiana Sports Hall of Fame in 1988 and elected to the College Football Hall of Fame in 1996.

My first piece of Pittsburgh Steelers memorabilia was a *Sports Illustrated* Terry Bradshaw poster that adorned my bedroom door when I was five years old. It is not hard to understand why the quarterback of a Super Bowl Dynasty would rate petty high on the cool-factor for a young fan. I was fortunate to begin following the Steelers at the pinnacle of Bradshaw's career, as he matured into one the greatest quarterbacks of all-time. It is well known that Bradshaw had his share of struggles and growing pains early in his career. Mistakes and miscues landed Bradshaw in Coach Chuck Noll's doghouse and led to him being benched in favor of quarterback Joe Gilliam. However, he worked his way back into the starting lineup, earned the confidence of his head coach and led Pittsburgh to their first Super Bowl championship in 1974. Bradshaw would go on to prove his detractors wrong and develop into one of the best big-game quarterbacks ever. He possessed a powerful throwing arm and was deadly accurate with his passing. His intelligence was famously called into question by the Cowboys' Thomas "Hollywood" Henderson prior to Super Bowl XIII. However, nothing could have been further from the truth. Bradshaw was entrusted to call his own plays while running the Steelers' offense. He had a remarkable ability to read defenses, and effectively and unselfishly mixed his running game with his passing attack to produce one of the most devastating offenses in league history. It is not a stretch to say that the Pittsburgh Steelers would not have been the Dynasty of the 1970s without Bradshaw as their quarterback.

Terry Bradshaw was drafted by the Pittsburgh Steelers with the first selection in the 1970 NFL Draft. The Steelers and the Chicago Bears had both finished the 1969 season with 1-13 records. Pittsburgh earned the right to draft Bradshaw by winning a tie-breaking coin flip. He played 14 seasons with the Steelers, winning four Super Bowl championships. He ended his career holding nearly every Steelers passing record. Bradshaw threw for 27,989 yards and had 212 passing touchdowns. He also recorded 32 rushing touchdowns in his career. However, it was in the Super Bowl where Bradshaw played his best. In four career Super Bowl games, he threw for 932 yards and had 9 passing touchdowns. Bradshaw was the MVP of Super Bowls XIII and XIV.

In his career, Terry Bradshaw was a three-time Pro Bowl selection, named First Team All-Pro in 1978, voted NFL Most Valuable Player in 1978, was *Sport Illustrated* Sportsman of the Year in 1979, named to the NFL 1970s All-Decade Team, voted to the Steelers' 50th Anniversary Team in 1982, named to the Steelers' All-Time Team in 2007 and was a member of the inaugural class of the Pittsburgh Steelers' Hall of Honor in 2017. Terry Bradshaw was inducted into the Pro Football Hall of Fame in his first year of eligibility in 1989.

Karen and I had obtained ten signatures on our helmet by the summer of 1996. We were extremely proud of what he had accomplished up to that point and happily displayed our helmet on the bookcase in our apartment. In late-August of 1996, my mother, Rose

Walter, and her friend, Robin Hinkleman, had planned a trip to visit their friends, Karen and Jim Summerville, who lived just outside of Dallas, Texas. Ironically, Terry Bradshaw was now living in the suburbs of Dallas, home of the hated Cowboys. The Summerville home was just a few miles from Terry Bradshaw's ranch. They had seen him from time to time at various community functions in their hometown, and the airport limousine was frequently seen driving to the Bradshaw home, presumably due to Terry's job with the *Fox NFL Sunday Pregame Show.*

For several weeks prior to my mother's trip, she had insisted that she could obtain Terry Bradshaw's signature on our helmet if we would allow her to take it on her trip to Texas. I simply laughed off the notion and told her she was crazy. However, after about the tenth time she nagged me about the helmet, I reluctantly consented. To be honest, I probably relented out of spite. I remember saying to her, sounding like the biggest smartass, "Sure, mom. You go get Terry Bradshaw's autograph." We put the helmet in a padded freezer bag and gave it to my mother to take to Dallas to have it signed by the Blond Bomber. All I could think was: Never going to happen!

My mother and Robin drove to Baltimore on a Thursday night and were scheduled to depart from BWI Airport the following morning. After arriving at their hotel, they decided to eat dinner at the hotel restaurant. My mother feared leaving the helmet in their room so she grabbed the bag and took it with her. Robin didn't initially understand the significance of the bag until my mother explained the story of its contents. For the remainder of the trip, Robin was a valuable protector of the bag. The following morning, my mother carried the bag through the airport. She heard the security staff comment about the football helmet that was in the bag as it passed through the screening area. She then carried the bag onto her flight to Texas, all the while hoping she wouldn't be pulled aside, questioned and arrested for trying to sneak a Pittsburgh Steelers helmet through enemy territory when she arrived at the Dallas/Fort Worth International Airport. Fortunately, she was not accosted by any fanatical Cowboys fans!

Upon arriving at the Summerville home on Friday afternoon, my mother explained her mission and requested to use their computer to type a letter to Terry Bradshaw. The Summervilles were happy to join in the quest and they hastily drafted a letter. Once completed, they immediately headed for the local post office. On the way, Karen stopped in front of Terry Bradshaw's ranch to copy down his street number for the letter. Once at the post office, my mother took out a black pen and addressed the envelope. However, neither of them knew the exact town in which Terry resided. He lived on the border of Keller and Roanoke, Texas, but Karen was unsure of the exact location. They left the town blank and approached the postal worker at the window. Karen asked the worker if she knew the town where Terry Bradshaw lived, and she responded, “Roanoke.” Karen picked up a blue pen at the window and filled in the town on the envelope and dropped the letter in the mailbox.

The weekend went by, and my mother wondered if her efforts were going to pay off. Meanwhile, back in Pennsylvania, Karen and I were trying not to think about the numerous disaster scenarios that we were sure were taking place. My mother, Karen, and Robin had gone shopping on Monday morning. In the early afternoon, Karen received a call from her husband, who was at home and had taken the week off during my mother’s visit. After an initial moment of shock, Karen handed her cell phone to my mother. Jim apologized for going through my mother’s purse, which she had left at the house, but Terry Bradshaw’s secretary had just called and said that he would be coming to his office, and if Jim wanted to drop off the helmet, Terry would be happy to sign it. The gold paint marker that had been used for each signature was at the bottom of my mother’s purse and Jim had hastily dumped the contents to find it. Terry’s secretary provided the address to his office and Jim drove there with the helmet and marker.

When he arrived, Terry’s secretary told Jim that she rarely opened his personal mail, but for some reason, after seeing the two different colors of ink on the envelope, she decided to open my mother’s letter. After reading it, she contacted Terry, who said that he would be glad to sign our helmet when he returned to the office that week. She also said that we had been fortunate that it had been raining in the Dallas area because Terry would likely have been on the golf course most of the week, and probably would not have been at the office during my mother’s visit. Jim left the helmet and his contact information with Mr. Bradshaw’s secretary, who stated that she would call after Terry signed it.

Tuesday and Wednesday went by and there was no call from Terry Bradshaw’s secretary. My mother began to get nervous, as the Labor Day Weekend was approaching and she would be returning home on Sunday. She told the Summervilles that if they had not heard anything by Friday morning, they would have to contact

Terry's secretary and pick up the helmet without his autograph. On Thursday morning, the ladies went to a local zoo for the day. That morning, Karen received another call from Jim. She handed the phone to my mother, and Jim told her that Terry's secretary had called and said that he had been busy all week, and he had to pick up the helmet without a signature. My mother sighed with dejection, only to have Jim laugh and say that he just picked up the helmet with a bold Terry Bradshaw autograph. I can only imagine how overjoyed my mother must have been, likely feeling a sense of pride in accomplishing just what she said she could do. My mother and Robin left for home on Sunday, having several great stories and memories to cherish with the Summervilles.

Upon returning to Pennsylvania, my mother drove directly to our apartment. As she entered the living room, she half heartily handed me the bag and stated that she was unable to obtain Terry Bradshaw's signature. Smugly, I kind of gave her the old "I told you so", and she asked me to check the helmet. As soon as I opened the bag, the first thing I saw was a gleaming gold Terry Bradshaw autograph on the front of our helmet. Apparently, my mother had already phoned Karen and told her the entire story, but they wanted the signature to be a surprise for me. Stunned, I turned to her as she smiled, with a tear of joy in her eye. All I could do was hug her and say that I would never doubt her again. It was truly a special moment for us, and my mother seemed to revel in having helped contribute to our quest. I hugged Robin, too, thankful for her role as the helmet's protector. Within minutes, I was on the phone with the Karen Summerville. I expressed my thanks and gratitude for her help in securing Terry Bradshaw's autograph. She was thrilled to play a part in our project. She handed the phone to Jim, who answered, "Terry Bradshaw's agent!" We shared a great laugh and I thanked him for all that he had done. We could never have completed our mission without Karen and Jim's help.

We could not be more thankful to my mother, and Robin, Karen, and Jim. They are all special people, and Robin and the Summervilles have been a part of my life since I was a young boy. It is an honor and a privilege to have them play such a huge role in our Super Steelers Journey. We will always have a special story to share together. I would also be remiss if I didn't give a special thank you to Terry Bradshaw's secretary, whoever she may be.

However, there is another interesting little story to come later regarding Terry's autograph on our helmet.

11

DONNIE SHELL

Donnie Shell was born in Whitmire, South Carolina on August 26, 1952. He was a four-sport athlete at Whitmire High School where he was an outstanding baseball player and linebacker on the football team. During his senior year, Shell captained a defensive unit that did not allow a single touchdown all season. He attended South Carolina State University, playing both football and baseball for the Bulldogs. He played three seasons at linebacker before switching to safety his senior year. Shell was named an All-American as a senior in 1973 and was an All-Mid-Eastern Athletic Conference selection. He was named to the Quarter Century Division II All-America Team in 1997. Shell was elected to the College Football Hall of Fame and the South Carolina State Hall of Fame in 1998. He was named to the South Carolina Football Hall of Fame in 2013 and the Black College Football Hall of Fame in 2015.

Shell was signed by the Pittsburgh Steelers as an undrafted free agent in 1974. The Steelers' 1974 draft class is legendary, with four Pro Football Hall of Fame members being selected in a single year. It can be argued that Donnie Shell should be the Steelers' fifth Hall of Famer from that incredible year. Shell was a starter at strong safety on the Steel Curtain Defense for more than a decade. He was nicknamed "The Torpedo" for his closing speed and willingness to launch himself into ball carriers who were often more than twice his size. This was never more evident than during a late-season game in 1978 against the Houston Oilers, and rookie running back Earl Campbell. Earlier in the season, Campbell had run over the Steelers' defense in a loss at Three Rivers Stadium. In the rematch in Houston, with the division title on the line, "The Torpedo" sank the rookie phenom. Early in the game, Campbell took a handoff off the right side and Shell unleashed a devastating hit that left the running back with injured ribs and a trip to the sidelines for the rest of the contest.

Shell was an invaluable contributor to the Steelers' four Super Bowl championships in the 1970s, and his resume is worthy of enshrinement in Canton. He played 14 seasons for the Steelers, seeing action in 201 games, which was second only to Mike Webster in the club's history when he retired in 1987. He recorded 51 interceptions and scored two career touchdowns. He held the NFL career record for interceptions by a strong safety at the time of his retirement. Shell was selected to five Pro Bowls, was a three-time First Team All-Pro, a member of the NFL Silver Anniversary Super Bowl Team, named to the Steelers' 50th Anniversary Team in 1982, voted to the Steelers' All-Time Team in 2007 and was a member of the inaugural class of the Pittsburgh Steelers' Hall of Honor in 2017.

Karen and I were excited when we learned that Donnie Shell would be attending an autograph event at the Camp Hill Mall on November 18, 1997. When we arrived for the signing, there was already a large crowd of fans gathered awaiting Donnie's arrival. As he made his way to the autograph area, the Steelers' fans erupted into a loud cheer. Donnie seemed to really enjoy interacting with the fans, and when we reached the autograph table, he greeted us with a big smile. We handed him our helmet and Donnie added a bold signature on the back. He handed the helmet back to us, gave us a handshake and thanked us for attending the event. It was a pleasure adding another Steel Curtain legend to our helmet.

12

CHUCK NOLL

Chuck Noll was born on January 5, 1932, in Cleveland, Ohio. He attended Benedictine High School where he was a running back and defensive tackle, winning All-State honors. He was named to the All-*Catholic Universe Bulletin* Team as a senior. Noll earned a football scholarship to the University of Dayton in 1949. He was named a co-captain at Dayton, where he played on the offensive line and at linebacker. He was elected as a charter member of the University of Dayton Athletic Hall of Fame in 1962. Noll was drafted by the Cleveland Browns in the 20th round of the 1953 NFL Draft. He played both offensive guard and linebacker under Hall of Fame coach Paul Brown, where he was a member of Cleveland's NFL Championship teams in 1954 and 1955.

Noll retired as a player after the 1959 season to begin his legendary coaching career. He was first hired by head coach Sid Gillman of the San Diego Chargers in the American Football League as a defensive line coach in 1960. He continued as defensive line coach until 1961 and was promoted to defensive coordinator and backfield coach in 1962, where he remained until 1965. During his six seasons as an assistant coach for the Chargers, Noll's teams appeared in five AFL Championship Games, winning the title in 1963. In 1966, Noll was hired by head coach Don Shula of the Baltimore Colts, where he was the defensive coordinator and backfield coach until 1968. Noll built a powerful defense in Baltimore, and the Colts won the NFL title in 1968 before being upset by the New York Jets in Super Bowl III.

It can be argued that the biggest key to the Pittsburgh Steelers' success in the 1970s was the hiring of Chuck Noll in 1969. Prior to Noll's arrival, the Steelers had never won a playoff game. Not long after he arrived, Pittsburgh became one of the greatest dynasties in all of sports. Noll's influence on the Steelers cannot be overstated. He was perhaps the game's best ever teacher, instilling fundamentals, discipline and a winning attitude that had never been present in Pittsburgh before he arrived. Noll was a master assessor of talent, not only finding and molding superstar players but seeing value in lesser known talent that others seemed to miss. He not only searched for talent at large, established colleges but also gave opportunities to players from smaller schools, often from predominantly African American colleges, which had not been routinely done before. The talent that the Steelers' accumulated through the draft in the early years of Noll's career in Pittsburgh is unprecedented. The Steelers routinely found valuable prospects and long-term contributors in late-round picks in the draft. Noll revolutionized how teams approached the NFL draft. He wanted players who fit the mold of Pittsburgh Steelers football. This is perhaps best exemplified by the fact that the 1979 Steelers' Super Bowl Championship team was made up entirely of players who had never played for another NFL team, which is not likely to ever be duplicated.

Chuck Noll coached the Pittsburgh Steelers for 23 seasons, accumulating a regular season record of 193-148-1. His career postseason record was 16-8, including a perfect 4-0 in Super Bowl games. Noll's teams won four Super Bowl titles, four AFC Championships, and nine AFC Central Division titles. He was named the UPI AFC Coach of the Year in 1972, voted the Maxwell Club NFL Coach of the Year in 1989, selected to the NFL 1970s All-Decade Team, named to the NFL 1980s All-Decade Team, elected to the NFL Golden Anniversary Super Bowl Team and was a member of the inaugural class of the Pittsburgh Steelers' Hall of Honor in 2017. The football field at Saint Vincent College in Latrobe, Pennsylvania, where the Steelers' have held training camp for decades, was renamed Chuck Noll Field in his honor in 2007. The City of Pittsburgh named a newly constructed street Chuck Noll Way in 2011. Chuck Noll was inducted into the Pro Football Hall of Fame in 1993. Sadly, Chuck Noll passed away in Sewickley, Pennsylvania on June 13, 2014, at the age of 82.

We were ecstatic when we found out that Chuck Noll would be making an autograph appearance at the Pennsylvania State Farm Show Complex on April 19, 1997. I, especially, was thrilled to meet the man that was affectionately crowned "Emperor Chaz" by Steelers' broadcaster Myron Cope, as he was the architect of the beloved teams from my childhood. It truly felt like we were in the presence of football royalty as we made our way to the front of the autograph line. While standing in the line, I began shaking our paint marker so that the ink would flow smoothly, but truth be told, it was more likely due to nervous energy and anticipation, as I was really looking forward to meeting Chuck Noll. We finally made it to the front of the line and Coach Noll greeted us with a smile and a hello, and we shared a brief conversation. I cannot recall what was said, as I'm sure I sounded like an awestruck rookie. We handed our helmet to Coach Noll and asked him if he would use our marker for the autograph. He took the marker and removed the cap, and then disaster struck. As soon as Coach Noll touched the helmet with the tip of the marker, paint exploded all over the side of it! I had apparently shaken the marker too long and the paint came out of it like water.

Do you remember that scene in *Saving Private Ryan*, when Tom Hanks is in shock, and in slow motion is surveying the beach at Normandy? That is kind of how I felt. I looked at Coach Noll and I will never forget the look on his face. He was absolutely stunned as to what had just happened and seemed to have lost his ability to speak. He didn't have to say anything. His expression conveyed how sorry he felt. Like Tom Hanks, I turned to further survey the scene. I wasn't completely sure that Karen was still breathing. She stood there with her mouth hanging wide open but was not taking in any oxygen. The gentleman sitting next to Coach Noll appeared to be in panic mode. As my senses began to return, I saw Coach Noll pick up a rag and attempt to wipe off the paint that was now running down the side of our helmet. When he saw how futile his attempt was to remove the paint, he picked up another marker and signed the helmet in a different spot. He handed the helmet back to me and we shared an unspoken farewell glance. Karen and I walked away from the autograph area to survey the damage.

There was a glob of smeared paint about 2-3 inches in diameter on the side of our helmet. However, trying to look at the situation with a "glass half full" outlook, somehow the paint managed to miss all of the other signatures, and it was on the back side of the helmet, where there was no logo. However, it appeared as though our project had come to an abrupt end. We had no idea how or if we could remove the paint without damaging the helmet. I remember thinking, "Well, at least we can display the signatures on the front of the helmet." Karen's apparent lack of oxygen at the time of the "eruption" didn't have a long-term effect. One of the things I love and admire most about her is her ingenuity. She had come up with her own solution.

The next day, I was watching television in our bedroom and in walked Karen with our helmet. The exploded paint was gone! For several hours, Karen had painstakingly removed the dried paint, flake by flake, with her fingernail. Incredibly, when she handed me the helmet, I could not tell the incident had even happened. The paint was completely gone. I couldn't believe it. In fact, another player later signed in the spot where the "Immaculate Explosion" occurred, and you would never know it happened. I owe Karen a lifetime of manicures, and if you look really close, she still might have some Super Steelers gold paint on her fingers. Happily, this is not our only memory of Chuck Noll. A few years later, we met him again at the Team of the Decade Reunion in Pittsburgh, and we obtained another autograph from Coach Noll, this time without incident.

Jack Ham

"Mean" Joe Greene

L.C. Greenwood

Lynn Swann

Dwight White

Rocky Bleier with Rose Walter

Rocky Bleier with Merrill and Karen

Mike Wagner

Dwight White teasing Karen

Jack Lambert

Merrill and Jack Lambert in 2017

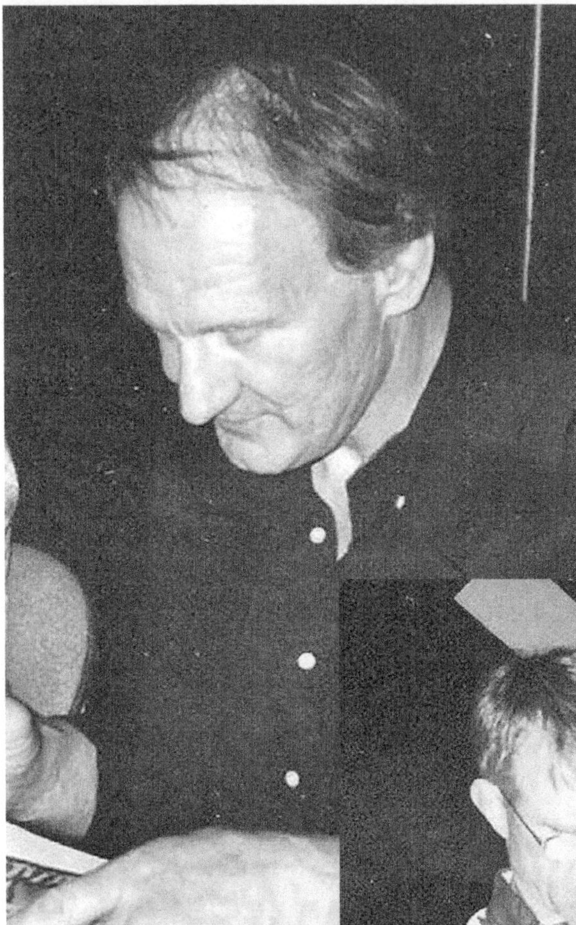

Mike Webster

Jon Kolb

Making things right with Ernie Holmes

J.T. Thomas

A special thank you for Terry Bradshaw

Question and answer session at the Team of the Decade Reunion in Pittsburgh

Chuck Noll

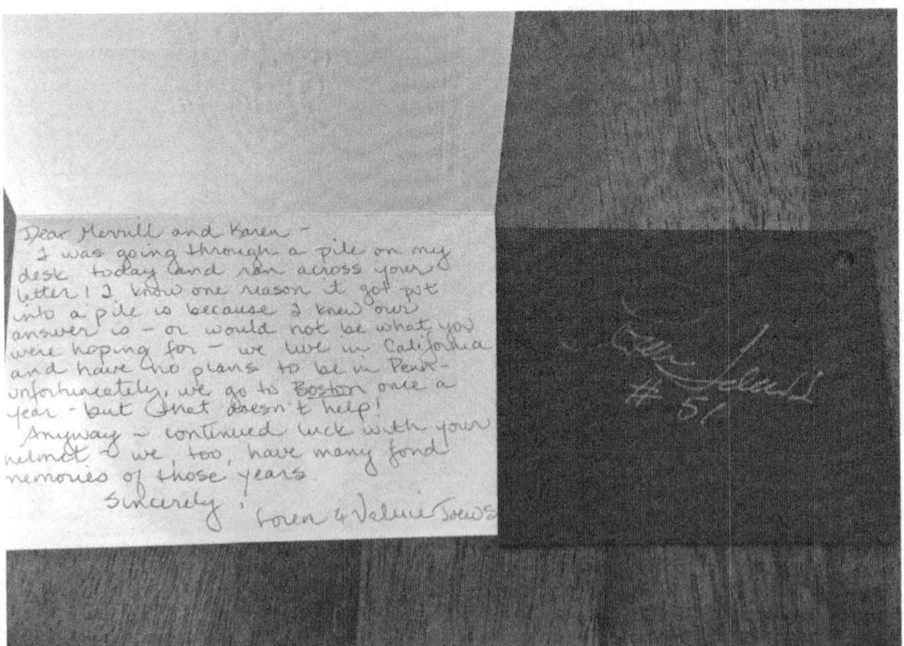

Dear Merrill and Karen -
I was going through a pile on my
desk today and ran across your
letter! I know one reason it got put
into a pile is because I knew our
answer is - or would not be what you
were hoping for - we live in California
and have no plans to be in Penn -
unfortunately, we go to Boston once a
year - but that doesn't help!
Anyway - continued luck with your
helmet - we, too, have many fond
memories of those years.
Sincerely,
Loren & Valerie Toews

#51

Original Loren Toews signature and letter

Loren Toews with the Walter Family

Loren Toews completing our Super Steelers helmet

Our Super Steelers helmet

Merrill, Lilly, and Karen with our Super Steelers helmet

13

STEVE FURNESS, RANDY GROSSMAN, LARRY BROWN AND GERRY MULLINS

Steve Furness was born in Providence, Rhode Island on December 5, 1950. He attended Bishop Hendricken High School. At Bishop Hendricken, Furness excelled in football and track and field. He earned a football scholarship to the University of Rhode Island in 1969. Furness was a First Team All-Yankee Conference selection in 1971. He not only starred in football with URI but also participated in the hammer throw as a member of the track team. His outstanding performance in the hammer throw earned Furness an invitation to the 1972 United States Olympic Trials. However, he turned down the invitation, as his abilities on the football field as a defensive lineman at URI caught the attention of the Pittsburgh Steelers, who chose him in the fifth round of the 1972 NFL Draft. Furness chose to forgo a possible place on the Olympic Track and Field Team to begin his NFL career with the Steelers. He was elected to the University of Rhode Island Athletic Hall of Fame in 1987. Furness was named to the Yankee Conference 50th Anniversary Team in 1996. In 1999, *Sports Illustrated* magazine named Furness as one of the 50 Greatest Rhode Island Sports Figures of the 20th Century, ranking him at #14.

Steve Furness is the kind of selfless player that every championship team needs on their roster. Furness' value to the Pittsburgh Steelers was proven in the fact that he earned four Super Bowl rings in his nine seasons with the team. Possessing tremendous strength and quickness at defensive tackle, he certainly earned his place amongst the Steelers legends. Never a superstar, Furness was a dependable backup to the star-studded Steel Curtain defensive line, who could be called upon to step into the starting lineup, when needed. He played in 106 regular season games for the Steelers and Detroit Lions, recording 32 career sacks and 8 fumble recoveries. Furness saw significant action in each of the Steelers' four Super Bowl victories, including starting at defensive tackle in Super Bowl XIII. Steve Furness was a reliable contributor to the success of the Steelers' dynasty teams in the 1970s.

Randy Grossman was born on September 20, 1952, in Philadelphia, Pennsylvania. He attended Havertown High School where he was a member of the football and wrestling teams. After a tremendous high school career, where he was All-State, All-League and All-County selections, Grossman accepted a football scholarship to attend Temple University. Grossman was an outstanding tight end for the Owls, earning All-East honors by the Associated Press as a junior in 1972. As a senior, he was named a Third Team All-American by the AP in 1973. He finished his career at Temple with 79 receptions, 1,505 receiving yards and scored 10 touchdowns. Grossman was elected to the Temple University Sports Hall of Fame in 1986. He was inducted into the National Jewish Sports Hall of Fame in 2013.

Grossman signed with the Pittsburgh Steelers as an undrafted free agent in 1974. The Steelers' 1974 draft class produced four Hall of Fame players, and although Grossman's career did not land him in Canton, he proved to be a valuable and key contributor to Pittsburgh's Super Bowl teams in the 1970s. He was an undersized tight end who made the most out of his eight seasons with the Steelers, earning four Super Bowl rings. Grossman possessed good speed and was a dependable receiver when targeted by Terry Bradshaw. His best season was in 1978 when he recorded a career-high 37 receptions, the most by a Steelers tight end in twelve years. He finished his career with 118 receptions for 1,514 yards and scored 5 touchdowns. Grossman was a clutch performer who caught a key touchdown pass to help secure Pittsburgh's victory in Super Bowl X. He is one of only two tight ends to win four Super Bowl rings, the other being Marv Fleming.

Larry Brown was born on June 16, 1949, in Jacksonville, Florida. He attended Bradford High School. After a stellar scholastic career, Brown earned a scholarship to the University of Kansas. Brown showed great athleticism and versatility at Kansas, playing multiple positions on both sides of the ball during his collegiate career. He was a defensive end as a freshman, switched to offensive tackle as a sophomore, returned to defensive end as a junior and moved to tight end as a senior. Brown helped lead the Jayhawks to the 1968 Orange Bowl. The Pittsburgh Steelers were impressed by Brown's career at Kansas and chose him in the fifth round of the NFL Draft in 1971.

Brown epitomized Coach Chuck Noll's motto for the 1970s Steelers: "Whatever it takes." He was a starter at two positions in his 14 seasons in Pittsburgh. He began as a tight end from 1971 until 1977, including two starts in the Steelers' first two Super Bowl victories. Fans will always remember Brown for his game-clinching touchdown catch in the waning minutes of Super Bowl IX, giving Pittsburgh its first World Championship. After the 1977 season, Chuck Noll asked Brown to switch positions and move to right tackle. The move paid off handsomely for the Steelers and Brown, as he played in two more Super Bowls, helping the team win titles in 1978 and 1979. Brown's versatility was an invaluable key to the Super Steelers success. He ended his career with 48 receptions, 636 receiving years and scored 5 touchdowns. Brown was named to the Pro Bowl in 1982. He was a member of the Steelers' 50th Anniversary Team in 1982 and was voted to Pittsburgh's All-Time Team in 2007.

Gerry Mullins was born in Fullerton, California on August 14, 1949. He excelled as a member of the football team at Anaheim High School and earned a scholarship to the University of Southern California. At USC, he was a member of three Rose Bowl teams as a tight end. He was selected by the Pittsburgh Steelers in the fourth round of the 1971 NFL Draft.

Mullins, or "Moon" as he would become known (nicknamed after the title character in the famous *Moon Mullins* comic strip), was an undersized guard, who made the most of his agility and quickness to play nine seasons with the Steelers, winning four Super Bowl championships. Lining up beside All-Pro centers Ray Mansfield and Mike Webster, Mullins used pulling and trap blocking to provide running lanes for Pittsburgh's perennial 1,000-yard rushers. The talent that Mullins displayed in college as a tight end also served him well in the NFL, as he had two career touchdown receptions for the Steelers. Pittsburgh fans will forever remember Mullins pulling on a sweep to the left and making a devastating block against linebacker Wally Hilgenberg, paving an uncontested path for Franco Harris to score against the Minnesota Vikings in Super Bowl IX. He is also remembered for recovering a key onside kick against the Dallas Cowboys in Super Bowl X. Mullins retired from football after the Steelers' victory in Super Bowl XIV, leaving the game as a four-time champion and a key contributor to the Steelers' Super Bowl Dynasty.

In 1997 there was a considerable amount of media attention focused on the upcoming 25th anniversary of the Immaculate Reception. That fall, we found out that several former Steelers would be taking part in a celebration of the famous play's silver anniversary. The celebration would take place on December 23, 1997, exactly 25 years to the day of the Immaculate Reception. The event was being held at the David L. Lawrence Convention Center in Pittsburgh, with players signing autographs for a donation to a local children's charity. Karen was unable to attend the celebration, but our friends, Troy Hoffman and Jeff Howe, were thrilled to make the trip and take part in the next chapter in our Super Steelers Journey. Not knowing exactly which players would be attending the event, we figured there would likely be a few that we needed for our Super Bowl helmet.

Troy, Jeff and I made the three-and-a-half-hour pilgrimage to Pittsburgh early in the morning on the day of the celebration. As we drove out the Pennsylvania Turnpike, Troy and I reminisced about our Super Steelers memories. Being a few years younger than us, and a Seahawks fan, we used the long drive to educate Jeff about the greatest football team of all-time. When we arrived at the convention center, we were amazed by the amount of media coverage the event was receiving, and the size of the crowd that had gathered. It was like a Steelers euphoria, with memorabilia and souvenirs galore. The actual football that Franco Harris scooped off the Three Rivers Stadium turf for the Immaculate Reception was on display at the event, and we got a close-up view of this Steelers Holy Grail. News crews were combing the venue, covering all aspects of the celebration. In fact, while we waited for the players to begin their autograph sessions, a crew came to the table where we were sitting and filmed Jeff holding our helmet. It marked the first time that our helmet received any media attention.

Eventually, several players made their way to the autograph area and began their signing sessions. As we approached the first player to sign our helmet, I felt like I had just seen a ghost. In the week prior to the celebration, Troy, Jeff and I were talking on the loading dock at work about the helmet and our excitement for the upcoming weekend. As we were talking, a little old man that I had never seen before approached us and said that he had overheard our conversation. Talking about our helmet, he said, "Too bad you'll never get my sister's boy." Puzzled, I looked at him and asked, "Who's your sister's boy?" He responded, "Steve Furness." I was admittedly disappointed with the sudden knowledge that we would never be able to complete our quest, and I said to the man, "I had no idea that Steve Furness had passed away. I guess we won't be able to complete our helmet." The man shook his head and walked out the door and we never saw him again.

At the celebration, I saw the man sitting at the first autograph table and couldn't believe my eyes. I looked at the name card on the table and it confirmed what I did not think was possible. Troy, Jeff and I just looked at each other in stunned disbelief. As I walked up to the table, Steve Furness greeted me with a smile and a hello. I must have had a strange look on my face, and I don't remember saying a word. I handed him our helmet and he signed a beautiful signature and his #64 on the back. He handed the helmet back to me, smiled, and wished me a Merry Christmas. I shook his hand, still speechless, and left the area to collect myself and try to figure out what had just happened. Troy, Jeff and I were just dumbfounded. Of all the players the little man could have mentioned, why did he say, "Steve Furness"? Obviously (and thankfully), he was mistaken, but this was certainly one of the more bizarre experiences in our journey. Sadly, Steve Furness died of a heart attack at the age of 49 on February 9, 2000, in Pittsburgh. He was the first of the 22 dynasty Steelers players to pass away. I am so honored and fortunate to have met Steve Furness before his passing, and every time I look at his signature I am reminded of our unforgettable encounter.

We continued to walk around the autograph area and discovered that Randy Grossman was in attendance. Randy was joyously interacting with the fans and reminiscing about his time with the Steelers. As I reached the table, Randy engaged me in a short conversation, thankfully giving me one of his infectious laughs. He signed our helmet on the front, just under Jack Lambert. He handed me the helmet with a firm handshake and wished us well. When I looked at his signature, I saw that Randy Grossman has one of the coolest autographs. Under his name, he placed four stars to signify each of the Steelers' four Super Bowl championships in the 1970s. Randy was definitely one of the most memorable players in our quest.

At the next table was Larry Brown. Larry was extremely nice and greeted me with a smile. He took our helmet and signed it on the back. I was wondering if he would sign it with a number, as he wore both #79 and 87. He chose #79, the number he wore as an offensive tackle and Pro Bowl selection. He gave me a firm handshake and wished us well.

Finally, we found that Gerry Mullins was in attendance at the celebration. Gerry seemed to enjoy interacting with the fans and greeted me with an enthusiastic smile and hello. He signed our helmet on the front and included his nickname "Moon". He handed me the helmet and wished us a Merry Christmas.

As Troy, Jeff and I left the celebration of the 25th Anniversary of the Immaculate Reception, we reveled in the great time we had and began the long drive home. Although we enjoyed seeing the players and all the memorabilia and loved the events at the celebration, the one thing we all agreed on was that each of us could now recite Jack Fleming's radio broadcast of the Immaculate Reception word for word, as it must have been replayed about 1,000 times throughout the day. But that play started the Steelers' dynasty, and no words were ever sweeter in Pittsburgh.

14

LYNN SWANN

Lynn Swann was born on March 7, 1952, in Alcoa, Tennessee. His family moved from Tennessee to San Mateo, California when he was two years old. Before Swann embarked on his legendary sports career, he was enrolled in dance classes at a young age. The skills he developed through ballet and tap dancing would later serve him well in athletics. Swann attended Junipero Sierra High School where he was a star in football, basketball, and track. He was the California State Champion in the long jump in 1970, outdistancing future Olympic gold medalist Randy Williams. Swann was a high school All-American wide receiver, and also played quarterback his senior season. He received the Junipero Sierra High School Hometown Hall of Fame honor in 2012. He accepted a football scholarship to the University of Southern California in 1970. Swann would go on to have a legendary collegiate career at USC. He was a member of the Trojans' undefeated National Championship team in 1972. Swann was a consensus All-American as a senior in 1973. He was named to the 1973 All-PAC Eight Team and was the USC team Most Valuable Player as a senior. Swann also won the 1973 Pop Warner Award as the best college football player on the Pacific Coast in 1973. He finished his collegiate career with 96 receptions, 1,562 receiving yards and scored 11 touchdowns. Swann was inducted into the USC Athletic Hall of Fame in 2005, named the Walter Camp Foundation Man of the Year in 1997, elected to the Bay Area Sports Hall of Fame in 2002 and voted to the Rose Bowl Hall of Fame in 2013. Lynn Swann was inducted into the College Football Hall of Fame in 1993. He also made a memorable appearance in 1981 on the children's television show *Mr. Rogers' Neighborhood*, talking about how his participation in dance helped him in his football career. Swann also talked with characters on the show to help children learn about competition and their feelings about winning and losing.

Swann was selected by the Pittsburgh Steelers in the first round of the 1974 NFL Draft. He made an immediate impact with the Steelers during his rookie year as a premier punt and kick returner. However, it would not take long for Swann to crack the starting lineup with his spectacular speed and leaping ability. Was there anything more beautiful on a football field than watching Swann floating through the air making an amazing catch? Swann made a routine catch look like a work of art. However, it was his pension for the sensational play that made him a legend. He turned *NFL Films* into his own personal highlight reel, and I remember being mesmerized as a boy watching the annual Steelers' season review with the great John Facenda narrating Swann's spectacular receptions. Although Swann played nine seasons with the Steelers, some experts argued that his career lacked longevity. However, no wide receiver in NFL history played bigger and had more memorable and historic moments on the game's biggest stage than Lynn Swann. All football fans remember Swann's "Kangaroo Catch" and "Levitating Leap" in Super Bowl X against the Dallas Cowboys, as they are shown in every highlight film, show or clip related to the history of the Super Bowl. In Super Bowl X, Swann had four receptions for a record 161 yards and a touchdown, earning Most Valuable Player honors. He scored the game-winning touchdown in the fourth quarter of Super Bowl XIII against the Cowboys. Swann also scored a touchdown in the Steelers' Super Bowl XIV victory against the Los Angeles Rams.

Swann finished his career with 336 receptions, 5,462 receiving yards and scored 51 receiving touchdowns. He had 72 rushing yards and scored one rushing touchdown. Swann accumulated 739 punt return yards and scored one touchdown. He totaled 48 receptions, 907 receiving yards and scored 9 touchdowns in postseason play, including 16 catches for 364 yards and 3 touchdowns in four Super Bowl games. Swann was the MVP of Super Bowl X, a three-time Pro Bowl selection, named a First Team All-Pro in 1978, voted NFL Man of the Year in 1981, selected to the NFL 1970s All-Decade Team, selected to the NFL Silver Anniversary Super Bowl Team, elected to the NFL Golden Anniversary Super Bowl Team, named to the Steelers' 50th Anniversary Team in 1980, selected to the Steelers' All-Time Team in 2007 and was a member of the inaugural class of the Pittsburgh Steelers' Hall of Honor in 2017. Lynn Swann was inducted into the Pro Football Hall of Fame in 2001.

On April 7, 1998, a celebration honoring the Most Valuable Players of the first 32 Super Bowls was held at the Garden State Expo Center in Somerset, New Jersey. For the first time ever, Lynn Swann was scheduled to make a public autograph signing. He would be appearing along with fellow Steelers' MVP's Terry Bradshaw and Franco Harris. Karen and I were extremely excited that Lynn was making a public appearance, and we were really looking forward to meeting him and adding his signature to our helmet. My mother joined us for the two-and-a-half-hour drive to the celebration, as she wanted to add Terry Bradshaw's signature to her collection. When we arrived at the Expo Center, we were utterly amazed at the gathering of so many football legends. In addition to our Steelers heroes, there were names like Starr, Namath, Dawson, Csonka, Montana, Rice, Young, Staubach, Aikman, Smith and on and on. It was a football lover's dream come true, but we were solely focused on the hero of Super Bowl X.

As we waited for Lynn's signing to begin, we were entertained by video screens featuring Super Bowl highlights, including many spectacular plays by Mr. Swann. Because this was Lynn's first public autograph signing, several hundred fans turned out to meet him in person. When we finally reached the autograph table, Lynn greeted us with a hello and a smile. I handed him our helmet and he searched for a spot to sign it. I pointed to an area on the front, near the bottom, and he happily added his signature. He shook our hands and wished us well, and we gleefully left the signing area to check out our newest autograph. Lynn's signature is every bit as graceful as his play on the field. The "S" in his last name takes the form of a swan, and it is one of the coolest and most unique autographs on our helmet.

On a side note, Karen and I accompanied my mother to Terry Bradshaw's signing at the celebration. This gave us the opportunity to thank him for signing our helmet, and my mother the chance to retell the entire story. We shared a laugh with Terry, and my mother gave him roses and a kiss on the cheek as tokens of her appreciation for the wonderful moments he had given us throughout his career and the unforgettable memories from her week in Texas in the summer of 1996.

15

JON KOLB, J. T. THOMAS, AND MIKE WAGNER

Jon Kolb was born in Ponca City, Oklahoma on August 30, 1947. He attended Owasso High School, where he was a standout football player. Kolb was an All-State offensive lineman his senior season, and he earned a football scholarship to Oklahoma State University in 1965. Kolb had a stellar collegiate career at Oklahoma State, earning All-Big Eight honors at center in 1967 and 1968. He was named an All-American in 1968. Kolb was elected to the Oklahoma State University Hall of Honor in 2001, the Pennsylvania Sports Hall of Fame in 2005 and the Oklahoma Sports Hall of Fame in 2009.

Jon Kolb was chosen by the Pittsburgh Steelers in the third round of the 1969 NFL Draft. He spent the next 13 seasons protecting quarterback Terry Bradshaw's blind side at left offensive tackle. Kolb possessed incredible strength and was considered one of the strongest men in the NFL during his career. He also had superior quickness and hand speed, enabling him to fend off pass rushers from the outside. He was equally proficient against the run, perfecting the Steelers' effective trap blocking schemes. Kolb was a key contributor to the Steelers' dynasty teams, starting every one of the team's playoff games during the 1970s, and only allowing one sack in Pittsburgh's four Super Bowl victories. Although he was never voted to a Pro-Bowl or All-Pro team, his importance to the Steelers' success was evidenced by his inclusion in club's 50th Anniversary Team in 1982, and Pittsburgh's All-Time Team in 2007. In addition to his outstanding football career, Kolb competed in the World's Strongest Man competitions in 1978 and 1979, finishing in the top five both years.

James Thomas, Jr., better known to Steelers fans as J.T. Thomas, was born on April 22, 1951, in Macon, Georgia. He was a stellar football player at Lanier High School, earning a scholarship to Florida State University in 1969. He would become the first African American football player at Florida State. Thomas had an outstanding collegiate career at cornerback and safety for the Seminoles. He set a school record with three interceptions in a single game in 1970. He was named a First Team All-American by *Pro Football Weekly* and *Time* magazine as a senior in 1972. Thomas was inducted into the Florida State University Hall of Fame in 1979 and was named to the Georgia Sports Hall of Fame in 2011.

J.T. Thomas was selected by the Pittsburgh Steelers in the first round of the 1973 NFL Draft. Thomas was a major contributor to Pittsburgh's Steel Curtain Defense for nearly a decade. Teaming with Mel Blount, Thomas became a member of one of the greatest cornerback tandems in history. NFL.Com named Thomas and Blount the sixth greatest cornerback combinations of all-time. Thomas was a fantastic athlete, capable of blanketing and shutting down opposing receivers with regularity. Thomas was an outstanding player in three of the Steelers' four 1970s Super Bowl victories. He contributed an interception of Roger Staubach of the Dallas Cowboys in Super Bowl X. Although he missed the entire 1978 season due to a rare blood disorder, Thomas was a four-time Super Bowl champion in his nine years with the Steelers. He was named to the Pro Bowl after the 1976 season. Thomas finished his career with 20 interceptions and scored 2 touchdowns.

Mike Wagner was born on June 22, 1949, in Waukegan, Illinois. He starred on the football team at Carmel High School and earned a scholarship to Western Illinois University. Wagner had a great college career as a defensive back and was a National Association of Intercollegiate Athletics (NAIA) All-American selection in 1969. He was inducted into the Western Illinois University Athletic Hall of Fame in 1976.

Players taken in the 11th round of the NFL Draft are not likely to make an NFL roster, let alone become a starter. But that is exactly what Mike Wagner did, becoming a key member of the Steelers' Steel Curtain Defense. Wagner came to the Steelers in 1971 and rapidly proved his worth. He was a quick, agile and aggressive safety, who became a starter in his rookie season, and was a fixture in the Steelers' secondary for the next decade. Wagner led the NFL with eight interceptions in 1973. He was an outstanding player in

Pittsburgh's four Super Bowl victories in the 1970s. He had key interceptions in Super Bowls IX and X, including a fourth-quarter pick of Dallas Cowboys quarterback Roger Staubach that helped the Steelers' increase their lead late in the game in Super Bowl X. Wagner finished his career with 36 interceptions and recovered 12 opponents' fumbles. He was named to the Pro Bowl in 1975 and 1976, and selected to the Steelers' 50th Anniversary Team in 1982.

A celebration of the Team of the Decade was held at the David L. Lawrence Convention Center in Pittsburgh from April 30-May 2, 1999. The weekend-long celebration coincided with the 25th anniversary of the Pittsburgh Steelers' first Super Bowl championship in 1974. Over 50 Steelers legends were scheduled to appear, including three players we needed for our Super Steelers project. Karen and I were extremely happy to see that Jon Kolb, J.T. Thomas, and Mike Wagner were scheduled to appear at the reunion. Again, my mother was all in for this Super Steelers celebration and we decided to take a mini-vacation and spend a long weekend in Pittsburgh. We stayed at a Marriott hotel near the convention center, which happened to be the same hotel where the Steelers' legends were also guests for the reunion. This only added to the fun and excitement of the weekend, as we were able to interact with many of the players in the lobby and at breakfast.

Jon Kolb, J.T. Thomas, and Mike Wagner were scheduled to sign autographs at the reunion on Saturday, May 1st. As we made our way to the convention center, the atmosphere on the reunion floor was just thrilling. There were exhibits of Steelers' team memorabilia and souvenirs and mementos from the team's glory days as far as the eye could see. It was amazing how casual the event was, and we freely talked and took pictures with several players. We had the chance to see the United States Postal Service's unveiling ceremony of the Pittsburgh Steelers' Decade of the 1970s postage stamp from the Celebrate the Century Series. We also were able to take part in a televised question and answer session with members of the Steelers' Dynasty teams, in which participants answered chosen questions that were submitted by fans that were in attendance. One of my questions was actually chosen and asked of Coach Chuck Noll during the filming of the session. I had asked Coach Noll what he said to the team in the locker room at halftime when the Steelers were unexpectedly trailing the Los Angeles Rams in Super Bowl XIV. He responded that he did not have to say much of anything. The team knew that they had not played up to expectations and they knew what corrections needed to be made. This was definitely one of the most enjoyable events during the course of our Super Steelers quest.

When the time came for our signings to begin, we proceeded to the autograph area. As we approached Jon Kolb, Karen remarked about how strong and fit he looked. She was not surprised when I told her about him competing in strongman competitions during his playing days, and that he had been strength and conditioning coach for the Steelers after his retirement. Jon greeted us with a hello, took our helmet and signed it on the front with his #55. He gave us an undoubtedly firm handshake and wished us well.

We next moved to J.T. Thomas' line. J.T. was well dressed in a shirt and tie and seemed to enjoy interacting with the fans. He greeted us with a smile and a hello, and then signed our helmet on the back with his #24. He shook our hands and thanked us for attending the reunion.

Mike Wagner was talking with each fan that approached him, and he seemed to revel in sharing stories from his playing days. He stood at his autograph table and greeted everyone with an enthusiastic handshake. Mike happily took our helmet and looked for a space to sign. As he was signing our helmet, Karen took a picture, with Mike sporting a sly grin, obviously enjoying his time at the reunion. He autographed the helmet on the back with his #23. He handed the helmet back to us and we thanked him for a memorable experience.

The Team of the Decade Reunion was a once in a lifetime event, and it was an experience we all will never forget. In addition to our helmet, we were able to obtain a cornucopia of Steelers memorabilia, photographs, and autographs. My mother scored several Steelers legends on a beautiful Team of the Decade print that was given out at the reunion. It was like being in Steelers Heaven, and we were sorry to see it come to an end.

There was an interesting side note from the reunion. We had previously written a letter to Mike Wagner, in care of the Steelers, in the fall of 1998, explaining our project and asking if there would be any way of obtaining his signature on our helmet. In August of 1999, we received a letter that was postmarked from Pittsburgh. When we opened the envelope, a note inside was written on "Michael J. Wagner" stationary. The note stated, "Dear Merrill and Karen, I'm sorry it took so long to respond. Ship helmet, insured, and include postage. I will autograph and return promptly. Best Regards, Mike."

Mike included his address and phone number. However, since we had sent our initial letter, Mike had signed our helmet at the re-union. This was a gracious and thoughtful gesture on his part, and we sent a response, thanking him for his offer. We included a copy of Karen's picture of him signing our helmet. We hope Mike enjoyed the image commemorating our special moment together.

16

SAM DAVIS

Sam Davis was born on July 5, 1944, in Jacksonville, Florida. He attended Northwestern High School where he excelled in scholastic football. Davis was a walk-on for the football team at Allen University and starred at offensive and defensive tackle, and also threw shot put and was a sprinter on the Allen track team. He was voted the Most Valuable Player of the football team and received All-Southwest Intercollegiate Conference First Team honors in 1966. Davis was elected to the Jacksonville Sports Hall of Fame in 1990 and was named #18 by the *Times-Union* (FL) of the Top 100 Athletes of the 20th Century in Jacksonville in 2000.

Every Super Bowl champion has its unsung heroes, and Sam Davis definitely fit that mold for the Pittsburgh Steelers. He was signed by the Steelers as an undrafted free agent in 1967. Davis became one of a handful of players who made the transition from the dreadful teams of the 1960s to the Super Bowl teams of the 1970s. After the arrival of Coach Chuck Noll in 1969, Davis went from a backup to the starting left guard on the Steelers' offensive line for the next decade. His quickness and strength enabled him to be equally effective on run blocking or pass protection. He teamed with Jon Kolb to form one of the most effective guard-tackle combinations of their era. Davis played 13 seasons for the Steelers and earned four Super Bowl rings. He was an invaluable contributor to the Steelers' Dynasty of the 1970s. Davis was named to the Steelers' 50th Anniversary Team in 1982.

Sam Davis' life after his playing career has not been without its challenges. In the early 1990s, he suffered from a debilitating brain injury that necessitated him being admitted into a personal care facility. After learning of his health issues, we doubted that we would ever be able to obtain Sam Davis' signature on our helmet and complete our project. To our shock, we saw an advertisement stating that Sam would be making an autograph appearance at the Monroeville Convention Center in Monroeville, Pennsylvania on September 21, 2002. We were thrilled at the possibility of meeting Sam and adding his signature to our helmet, and we prayed he would be healthy enough to attend the event. We thought that this may be our only opportunity to have him sign our helmet. Karen was unable to attend the autograph signing, so my mother happily accompanied me to Monroeville to meet Sam Davis.

Upon entering the convention center, we were assured that Sam Davis would be in attendance that afternoon. When he arrived, Sam was assisted to the autograph area. As we approached the autograph table, Sam appeared to enjoy interacting with the fans, but sadly, he certainly seemed to have some severe limitations. When we reached the front of the line, an assistant helped Sam hold our helmet and he added his signature on the back. As he handed the helmet back to me, he gave us a warm smile and I thanked him for making the time to attend the event. I told him that it was truly an honor to meet him and he was a treasured addition to our Super Steelers helmet.

17

LOREN TOEWS

Loren Toews was born in Dinuba, California on November 3, 1951. He attended Del Mar High School where he was an outstanding football player. Toews earned a scholarship to the University of California at Berkley in 1969. He was a star on the Bears' defense and was a two-year letterman in 1971 and 1972. Toews received the Stub Allison Award in 1972, given to the team's Most Inspirational Player. In addition to his success on the gridiron, Toews was a member of Cal's rugby team. He was a starter on the Bears' squad that toured Australia and New Zealand for six weeks in 1971, posting a record of 6-3 against world-class competition.

Toews was selected by the Pittsburgh Steelers in the eighth round of the 1973 NFL Draft. An outstanding athlete and gifted linebacker, Toews could always be counted on to make timely plays and do whatever it took to help the Steelers win. Although he spent most of his career backing up the likes of Hall of Famers Jack Ham and Jack Lambert, Toews was a major contributor to the Steelers' success in the 1970s. Starting in Super Bowl XIII, Toews saw significant playing time in each of Pittsburgh's championship games. Toews played eleven seasons with the Steelers, earning four Super Bowl rings. He saw action in 149 regular season games, intercepted four passes, recovered ten opponents' fumbles, recorded two and a half quarterback sacks and was credited with two safeties.

While playing for the Steelers, Toews earned his MBA from the University of Pittsburgh's Graduate School of Business. After retiring from football, he and his brother, Jeff Toews, formed their own real estate company in San Jose, California. Jeff Toews also played in the NFL as an offensive lineman for the Miami Dolphins. Jeff Toews participated in Super Bowls XVII and XIX with the Dolphins. Between the two of them, the Toews brothers appeared in six Super Bowls. The Toews family certainly has a winning pedigree, and this not only was evident on the football field but in the business world, as well.

By 1997, our Super Steelers helmet was nearly complete. One of the few signatures we were missing was Loren Toews. To our knowledge, he had never appeared at any autograph signings, nor had he participated in any of the prior Steelers' reunions or functions. Desperate to complete our project, we decided to write a letter to Loren. We explained our project and asked him if he ever participated in any public autograph functions, or if there was any way we could possibly meet with him if he was ever near our area. Not knowing Loren's home address, we sent the letter in care of the Pittsburgh Steelers and hoped for a response.

Two years went by and there was no response to our letter. We figured that Loren likely never received it and we continued to search for any events where he may be present. However, in April of 1999, we received an envelope postmarked from San Francisco, California, with a return address from Pittsburgh. We hastily opened the envelope and saw that it contained a letter on Loren Toews' personal stationery. The letter was a personal note from Loren and Valerie Toews, apologizing for how long it had taken for them to respond. Our initial letter had actually been forwarded to the Toews' by the Steelers, but it had apparently been mixed in with a pile that had sat for a long time on Loren's desk. The Toews' letter was bittersweet, as it was exciting to receive a personal response, but stated that they lived in California and had no plans to visit Pennsylvania. They wished us luck with our helmet, and Loren actually autographed a piece of black construction paper in gold ink. In the upper right corner of the paper, they had punched a hole and tied a gold ribbon. We assumed that the ribbon was to tie the autograph to the facemask so that if we never had the opportunity to meet Loren, we would at least have his signature to display with our helmet. The letter and autograph were extremely kind and thoughtful gestures, but we were admittedly disappointed. We decided to continue on with our search and held out hope that we would someday cross paths with Loren and obtain his signature on the helmet.

Over the next several years, Karen and I continued a near weekly search of Pittsburgh Steelers events where Loren might appear. We even found his home address through a fellow collector, who had obtained Loren's autograph through the mail. Although having Loren's address was helpful, we didn't want to risk sending our helmet, unsolicited, through the mail and hope for a positive outcome. We also wanted to respect Loren's privacy and did not want to be a nuisance. Sam Davis had been the last player to sign our helmet in 2002, and at times, it seemed like our project would never be complete. However, we refused to give up all hope.

Karen and I watched the Steelers play the New Orleans Saints on television on November 30, 2014. It was alumni weekend for the Steelers, and there was an on-field ceremony honoring the 40th anniversary of the team's first Super Bowl championship. As the camera scanned the players standing on the sideline, I swore I saw one of them wearing a #51 jersey. I shouted to Karen that I thought I had seen Loren Toews standing on the sideline at Heinz Field. We both doubted that the player was Loren Toews, as he had never taken part in any past reunions. I pulled out my cell phone and immediately logged into the Steelers' website. There had been a banquet the previous evening honoring the 1974 team. The dinner had been open to the public, and unbelievably, Loren Toews had attended. I was stunned. That meant that the player I had seen on the sidelines at Heinz Field was indeed Loren Toews. We had missed the only opportunity to possibly meet Loren at a public event, and he was now standing in Pittsburgh, a mere three-and-half-hour drive away. Karen exclaimed, "If you can get someone from the Steelers to hold him there, I'll drive there right now!" We were sickened at this lost opportunity, as we scrolled through pictures from the previous night's banquet on the Steelers' website. Again, we questioned whether or not we would ever complete our Super Steelers helmet.

We were visiting my mother on Easter weekend in the spring of 2017. As we were returning from taking her out for lunch, she asked if we could stop and drop off a package at her brother's home. She did not expect anyone to be home, so we figured we would drop off the package and leave. However, when we pulled in, my uncle's truck was parked in the driveway. We decided to stop for a short visit.

To our surprise, not only was my uncle, Larry Walter, home, but his son, Brian, and grandson, Chase were visiting from Erie, Pennsylvania. We went inside and chatted in the living room. Being from Erie, Brian and his family are tremendous Steelers fans. Naturally, our conversation steered towards the Steelers and the prospects for the upcoming season. Somehow, the subject switched to our helmet, which Brian had never heard about before. When we mentioned that we were only missing Loren Toews' signature, and he lived in San Jose, both Brian and Chase looked at each other. Chase pulled out his cell phone and logged into Google Maps. He showed the phone to Brian, who said, "You know, we're taking a vacation to California in June." Karen and I were both stunned and intrigued. He said that they would be near San Jose on the last day of their trip, and if we could somehow contact Loren Toews, they would be happy to take our helmet with them to California. We were now elated and agreed to take Brian up on his offer. The only problem was we had to try to contact Loren Toews and hope for a positive response.

A few days after our meeting with Brian, we decided to try writing another letter to Loren Toews. This time, however, we could contact him directly, as we now had his home address. We wrote in the letter that my cousin and his family would be visiting California in June, and he would be in the San Jose area on June 20th. I thanked him for his response and autograph back in 1999, but said that we would be grateful if there would be some way that Loren could meet Brian during their visit. I provided my home and cell phone numbers, home address and included a self-addressed stamped envelope to aid Loren in a possible response. Karen mailed the letter and we crossed our fingers.

About a week after mailing our letter, I checked the mail when I arrived home from work. My heart began to pound as I saw our self-addressed envelope in the mailbox. I took the envelope inside and sat on the couch. For several minutes, my thoughts raced about what was inside. I wondered if Loren responded that he couldn't meet with Brian, but then thought that if the response was negative, why would he respond at all. I knew that whatever was inside the envelope would likely once and for all make or break our Super Steelers project. I held my breath, did a sign of the cross and tore open the envelope. When I read the note inside, I nearly had tears in my eyes. But these were tears of joy. Loren's wife, Valerie, had written a response, stating that she thought it would be best if Brian contacted her a few days prior to arriving in San Jose, and she would make the arrangements for him to meet with Loren. Valerie included her cell phone number and said that the meeting would likely take place at a local Starbucks coffee shop. It seemed almost impossible to believe that our long journey may be coming to an end. I immediately called Karen and told her the wonderful news and she was absolutely thrilled. I sent Brian a text message and informed him of Valerie Toews' response. He was excited to take part in our Super Steelers project, and I forwarded Valerie's contact information. Brian picked up the helmet at my mother's home on Mother's Day weekend, and we all prayed that everything would come together.

Brian and his family (wife, Angela, son, Chase and daughter, Emily) boarded a flight to California on June 12, 2017. He carried the helmet in the same bag that my mother used to travel to Texas. There were no issues whatsoever taking the bag through security and carrying it onto their flights. After arriving in California, the Walters' rented a car and drove to the hotel where they would be staying for the first leg of their trip. As they arrived at the hotel, Brian asked Angela if she thought they should take the helmet inside the hotel with them, or lock it in the trunk of the car and provide the staff with the valet key. They debated for a few moments as they approached the valet area, and at the last second, decided to take the helmet with them. This seemingly insignificant decision proved to be a wise one. The next day, as the family prepared to leave the hotel for the first excursion of their trip, they were informed by the hotel's management that the keys to their vehicle had been misplaced, and the rental company was providing them with a replacement. The keys to the original vehicle were never actually found, and had they decided to lock the helmet in the car, they would have had to contact a locksmith to open the trunk.

As Brian and his family traveled each day and made their way through central California, they took the helmet with them, not wanting to risk leaving it at their hotel. This caused additional concerns, as there were days when the outside temperature approached 100 degrees. Brian worried that the extreme temperatures might cause the paint of the signatures to become tacky and damage the helmet. As a result, every time they got into their vehicle, they opened the bag to check the helmet. Fortunately, the signatures held up just fine.

The entire time the Walters' were in California, we never heard from them. There were several times leading up to June 20th that we were tempted to contact them for an update. We wondered if Brian was able to contact Valerie Toews, if they were going to be able to meet with Loren and if anything had gone wrong. However, we did not want to interrupt their trip and detract from their time together. We agreed that no news was good news and refrained from contacting them. Brian would later tell me that they purposely did not contact us, wanting the meeting with Loren to be a surprise. In fact, Brian was in constant contact with Valerie and the meeting had long been arranged for when they arrived in San Jose.

On June 20th, the Walters' made their way to San Jose. However, they were arriving later in the day than originally expected. Brian contacted Valerie, who suggested that they meet Loren at his real estate office, rather than at the Starbucks store, as originally planned. Unfortunately, Valerie would not be available to meet the Walters', as she was preparing for a family function that weekend. When the Walters' arrived at Loren's office, he greeted them and welcomed them inside. The family briefly talked with Loren about their vacation, and about our helmet. We had given Brian a few of Loren's football cards to have signed for themselves as mementos from their trip, and he used them as kind of a warm-up for the helmet. As Loren took the helmet, Brian, Angela, Chase, and Emily all used their cameras to take pictures and video of this wonderful event. Loren searched the helmet for a space to sign, humorously commenting about the size of Jack Ham's signature. He found a spot on the front of the helmet, just under Jack Lambert's autograph. Loren practiced his signature in the air and then emblazoned the helmet with his autograph and his #51. In that brief moment, a 23-year quest had come to a joyous end. Loren had a wonderful smile on his face and Brian thanked him for completing our Super Steelers helmet. The Walters' took several pictures with Loren to commemorate the moment, and they happily left his office with memories to last a lifetime.

Meanwhile, it was approximately 6:00 pm back in Pennsylvania, and we were waiting with baited breath. All of a sudden, I heard a ding from my cell phone. I frantically checked for the message, and Brian had texted a picture of the Walters' posing with Loren and our completed helmet. I instantly felt overjoyed and had a feeling of total satisfaction. I immediately called Brian and he detailed their entire trip, including their interaction with Valerie and their time with Loren. I could not thank them enough for what they had done for us, and we looked forward to seeing them upon their return home. They arrived back in Erie the next day, with the helmet safe and sound, and now finished.

Brian delivered the helmet to my mother about a week after their trip, and she brought it to our home a few days later. It took several days for us to put it back in the custom case where it is stored in our office, as we could not stop admiring our completed project. We had a chance to visit with the Walters' over the July 4th holiday and they told us numerous stories about their trip and their time with Loren. We, again, expressed our gratitude to the Walters' for everything they had done to make our Super Steelers helmet a reality. We are honored that they are a part of this remarkable story. We could have never completed our quest without them, and they will always hold a special place in our hearts.

After Loren Toews completed our helmet, we contacted Valerie to thank them for their kindness and generosity. She responded, stating that we now had a special piece of history, and she was happy that our project was now complete. Valerie actually thanked us, and Brian, for being so kind during the entire process. That struck me as incredibly gracious. They had given us, a couple of Steelers fans whom they had never met, very special gifts of their time and personal interaction, and it is us who are eternally grateful. Loren and Valerie are kind, thoughtful and giving people, and we could not have asked for a better way to complete our Super Steelers journey. Our only regret is that we didn't have the chance to meet the Toews' in person. We sincerely hope that our paths will cross someday.

18

THE AGONY OF AUTHENTICITY

After our wonderful quest had finally come to an end, we felt that it would be wise to have the signatures on our helmet authenticated for insurance purposes. Although we knew that the autographs were genuine, having a letter of authenticity from a reputable company would verify that the signatures were legitimate if they were ever called into question. There are two companies who are recognized as the leaders in autograph authentication; James Spence Authentication (JSA) and Professional Sports Authenticators (PSA). Although both companies offer authentication services through the mail, we were hesitant to ship our helmet, as it has obvious sentimental value, and it could never be replaced. We had previously seen both companies doing authentications at sports card shows and conventions, and at local hobby shops, so we decided to check their online schedules for any possible appearances near our area. As luck would have it, JSA was going to be attending a sports card convention in Valley Forge, Pennsylvania in late-September, so we marked our calendar for the event.

I packed up our helmet drove to the Valley Forge Resort on September 24, 2017. I found JSA's booth at the convention and spoke with one of the authenticators. I expressed our concern about shipping the helmet through the mail, and the gentleman said that they would be able to authenticate the signatures in about two hours at the convention. He said that the price was $150, pass or fail, and a letter of authenticity or denial would be sent within two weeks. I was thrilled that the authentication could be done while I waited, and $150 seemed like a reasonable price to verify the signatures. I agreed to have JSA authenticate our helmet and completed their submission form. I took our helmet out of the bag and placed it on the table, and the authenticator commented how nice it looked. The gentleman said that he did not need any assistance identifying the players who had signed the helmet, nor did he want any form of verification. He stated that JSA had an extensive database of each of the players' signatures and they would analyze each one against their examples. Obviously, I had no doubt that each of the signatures was genuine, so I took my bag and went to roam the convention floor until the process was complete. However, before I left the booth, the authenticator asked, "Where did you get the Bradshaw?" Puzzled, I responded and told him the story of my mother's trip to Texas. He did not have much of a response and then said that I could check back at the booth in about two hours. I have to admit, his question left me a little uneasy.

I spent the next two hours walking around the convention. I don't remember much from the displays of memorabilia. My mind was racing, wondering why the authenticator was questioning Terry Bradshaw's signature. I kept inconspicuously walking past JSA's booth to see if they might have completed their examination and if I could get any sense of where things stood. Time seemed to stand still, and the authenticator actually took more than the two hours to complete his assessment. Finally, I noticed that our helmet had been moved from the authentication table and I immediately returned to JSA's booth. The authenticator handed me the helmet and had me sign a form stating that I had picked it up. As I signed the form, he did not say a word about their examination, so I finally asked how the authentication went. The gentleman said that all of the signatures were genuine, but they were questioning the Terry Bradshaw autograph. My heart began to pound and I immediately felt sick to my stomach. When I asked him why they were questioning the signature, he said that there are known secretarial examples of Terry Bradshaw's autograph in the marketplace. I now was in a full-blown panic. Terry Bradshaw's signature was the only one that no one had actually witnessed, and our helmet was dropped off with his *secretary*. The authenticator said that Terry Bradshaw's autograph has changed dramatically over the years and it can be tricky to verify. He said that they had taken pictures of the signature on our helmet and they intended to do further research at their home office in New Jersey. He told me that we would receive our letter in about two weeks.

As I left the convention and walked back to my car, I was in a daze. I immediately called Karen. She could not believe what was happening. After all the time, effort and commitment, the wonderful stories and the remarkable people who helped make our Super Steelers quest a reality, how could the biggest name on our helmet be a fake? And we now had to wait two weeks to find out the fate of our project? The emotional rollercoaster was brutal. Over the next two weeks, I went back and forth about a 1,000 times as to whether or not Terry Bradshaw's signature was legitimate. I looked at dozens and dozens of photos online of Bradshaw autographs that had been deemed authentic by JSA. Some looked just like the signature on our helmet, some did not. I kept trying to rationalize the situation. I said to myself that my mother's story was rock solid, and if Terry Bradshaw wasn't going to sign our helmet, there would be no way that his secretary would sign it in for him. However, I also kept coming up with moments of doubt. It got so ridiculous that I started questioning the # sign under Bradshaw signature. With nearly all of the genuine Terry Bradshaw autographs I had seen, he either signed just his name, or he signed his name and just his number. He never seemed to use the # sign. However, our helmet had his signature and #12 under his name. Well, I thought, that definitely means it's a fake. This back and forth inner drama went on for 16 long days.

On October 10, 2017, I returned home from work and noticed a large envelope on top of our mailbox. I knew exactly who the envelope was from, and I broke out in a nervous sweat. As I approached the mailbox, I saw JSA's logo on the return address. I took the letter inside, sat on the couch, did a Hail Mary and ripped open the envelope. I must have scanned over the letter about 100 times in 30 seconds. The first word that stuck out was "AUTHENTIC". The word I did not see was "SECRETARIAL". As my pulse rate began to recover, I was able to read the entire letter, which stated that all of the autographs on our helmet were deemed to be authentic, including the Terry Bradshaw. The only thing I could say was Thank, God! I immediately called Karen and told her the wonderful news. She let out a sigh of relief, as she admitted that she was not as calm and collected as she appeared to be during the past two weeks. Although the whole ordeal had been extremely stressful, I could not help but applaud James Spence Authentication for doing their due diligence and not just rubber stamping our Terry Bradshaw autograph as genuine or secretarial. They did exactly what we had hired them to do, and it was the best $150 we could have spent.

19

A VERY HAPPY AND APPRECIATIVE ENDING

It is hard to describe the range of feelings and emotions that we have felt during this long, strange, crazy and wonderful 23-year journey. They have ranged from frustration, anxiety, anxiousness, sadness and hopelessness to happiness, exhilaration, love, gratitude, and pride. When Karen and I began our Super Steelers helmet, we had no idea the crazy twists and turns we would experience along the way. However, the most enjoyable and satisfying result of this quest was sharing it with all the wonderful people who became a part of our story.

I cannot imagine my life without Karen Shaffer. She is my rock, the love of my life and my best friend. I am so fortunate to have shared the past 23 years of marriage with her, and I am blessed to share our loving home with our daughter, Lilly. When I think of the 23 years we spent working together on this project, it was truly a labor of love. One of the reasons that we cherish our helmet is that it represents a timeline of our lives together, through our engagement, marriage, anniversaries and the arrival of our daughter. Beyond a piece of sports memorabilia, it is a time capsule in the lives of the Shaffer family, and there is nothing but happy and joyous memories in that beautiful Steelers helmet.

There is no way that we could have completed a project of this magnitude without the help of so many remarkable people. Again, when we look at our helmet, we are reminded of all our family and friends with whom we had the pleasure of sharing this magical experience. From Texas to New Jersey to Monroeville to Pittsburgh, my mother, Rose Walter, played a loving and integral role in our journey. She is a diehard Pittsburgh Steelers fan, who always believed in what we were trying to accomplish and encouraged us to never give up on our pursuit. She willingly and enthusiastically participated in helping us acquire our Super Steelers autographs. She shared in our joy as we added each new signature. Our helmet reminds us of the love we share with her, and it will always serve as a reminder of the special bond that we have together.

Our helmet also reminds us of special people who, in one way or another, were a part of this wonderful story. Friends like Jim and Karen Summerville, Robin Hinkleman, Troy Hoffman and Jeff Howe were invaluable to the success of our quest, and we could have never achieved our goal without their help. Robin's husband, Gary Hinkleman, also shared in the joy of the journey and provided unwavering support.

Michael Bell played an "Immaculate" role in our Super Steelers helmet. Every time we look at Franco Harris' signature, we see Mike's smiling face and a playful wink. Although Mike is no longer with us, there is something magical about our helmet. His spirit and kindness live on every time it is shared and enjoyed.

My father and stepmother, Merrill and Debbie Shaffer, my brother and his wife, Jason and Karen Shaffer, and Karen's brother and his wife, Bob and Marie Travitz, all offered support and encouragement at each step of our journey.

Countless friends and co-workers at Feeser's Food Distributors were constantly on the lookout and informed me of player appearances, knowing that we were always searching for Super Steelers for our helmet. Linda Waller, Don Acker, Matt Bryner, Aida Cruz, Bob Dungan, Angela Livingston, Scott MacDerment, Jason Soboleski, Alison Vazquez, Derek Warner, Tony Woods and the rest of my friends and co-workers at Lancaster County Adult Probation and Parole Services were a non-stop source of encouragement, routinely prompting me to seek the final signature for our helmet and celebrating with us when we finally secured it. Our helmet serves as a constant reminder of these special people.

We are forever indebted to Brian, Angela, Chase and Emily Walter. They brought this long journey to a wonderful conclusion. We are thrilled that they all are now a part of our helmet's story. Their willingness to take time out of their vacation to California, contact Valerie Toews and make the arrangements to meet with Loren and ultimately complete our quest were acts of kindness that we will never forget. Words could never express the gratitude we have for them, and we are so proud to call them family. Their spirit and love will always be a part of our Super Steelers helmet.

Valerie Toews is one of the kindest, most sincere and gracious people we have ever known. Our Super Steelers journey could never have come to such a memorable end without her. We can never thank her enough for giving of her time and effort in responding to our request, making the arrangements for the meeting between the Walters' and Loren, and understanding just how much it meant to us to complete this wonderful project. Happily, we have remained in contact with Valerie and she is truly a remarkable person. Loren's signature is boldly displayed on the front of our helmet, and when we look at it, we will always think of Valerie Toews with a fond and appreciative smile.

The Pittsburgh Steelers have been a special part of my life since I was a child. From the 1970s until today, I have spent my Sunday afternoons in the fall with the Steelers. They have become ingrained into the fabric of my life. I cheer on the current team with the same enthusiasm and spirit that I had as a young boy, and I hope and pray each season brings another Lombardi Trophy to the City of Pittsburgh. However, the Super Steelers of the 1970s, the teams that I so fondly remember from my childhood, will always hold a special place in my heart. The 1970s Pittsburgh Steelers were the greatest dynasty in football history. Those teams, and more specifically, those players and coaches, provided me with some of the happiest moments of my life. Those memories are so vivid; I can still see them as if they just happened yesterday. Watching my heroes in Black and Gold brought me nothing but happiness and joy in my life, and perhaps that is why we decided to start this quest and find a way to honor them. The 23 men who have signed our helmet mean the world to me. It has been my honor to help create something special to commemorate this remarkable team. Our Super Steelers helmet reflects tradition, joy, and happiness, and it will always serve as a loving tribute to the men who signed it and those who helped make it happen. Here we go Steelers, here we go!! Thank you, one and all.

REFERENCES

CHAPTER 2

Cfbhall.com (College Football Hall of Fame)
Gopsusports.com (Penn State University Athletics)
Pabook.libraries.psu.edu (Pennsylvania Center for the Book)
Polishsportshof.com (National Polish-American Sports Hall of Fame)
Profootballhof.com (Pro Football Hall of Fame)
Pro-football-reference.com (Pro Football Statistics)

CHAPTER 3

Kentstatesports.com (Kent State University Athletics)
Profootballhof.com . . . (Pro Football Hall of Fame)
Pro-football-reference.com (Pro Football Statistics)
Si.com (Sports Illustrated)

CHAPTER 4

Archive.sportingnews.com (The Sporting News)
Blackpast.org (African American History)
Collegian.psu.edu (Daily Collegian, Penn State University News)
Pabook.libraries.psu.edu (Pennsylvania Center for the Book)
Pasportshof.org (Pennsylvania Sports Hall of Fame)
Profootballhof.com (Pro Football Hall of Fame)
Pro-football-reference.com (Pro Football Statistics)

CHAPTER 5

Cowboysofcolor.org (National Multicultural Western Heritage Museum and Hall of Fame)
Georgiaencyclopedia.org (State of Georgia History)
Lasportshall.com (Louisiana Sports Hall of Fame)
Pasportshof.org (Pennsylvania Sports Hall of Fame)
Profootballhof.com (Pro Football Hall of Fame)
Pro-football-reference.com (Pro Football Statistics)

CHAPTER 6

Exhibits.library.unt.edu (University of North Texas)
Meanjoegreene75.com (Joe Greene)
Profootballhof.com (Pro Football Hall of Fame)
Pro-football-reference.com (Pro Football Statistics)

Sports.jrank.org (Athlete Search)
Tisd.com (Temple Independent School District)
Wacotrib.com (Waco Tribune-Herald Newspaper, Waco, Texas)

CHAPTER 7

Helmehut.com (Football History)
Huddleupforkids.org (Huddle Up for Kids Foundation)
Pro-football-reference.com (Pro Football Statistics)
Rockybleier.com (Rocky Bleier)
Xavierhawkssports.com (Xavier High School Athletics)

CHAPTER 8

Al.com (State of Alabama News)
Biographyarchive.com (Celebrity Biography)
Encyclopediaofalabama.org (State of Alabama History)
Johnstallworth.com (John Stallworth)
Mrowl.com (Community Interest Search)
Profootballhof.com (Pro Football Hall of Fame)
Pro-football-reference.com (Pro Football Statistics)
Rd.com (Readers Digest)
Thehodagheadlines.com (Rhinelander High School Student News)
Uwbadgers.com (University of Wisconsin Athletics)
Wifca.org (Wisconsin Football Coaches Association)
Wihalloffame.com (Wisconsin Athletic Hall of Fame)

CHAPTER 9

Lcgreenwood68.com (L.C. Greenwood)
Lionathletics.com (Texas A&M University-Commerce Athletics)
Pasportshof.org (Pennsylvania Sports Hall of Fame)
Profootballhof.com (Pro Football Hall of Fame)
Pro-football-reference.com (Pro Football Statistics)
Profootballresearchers.org (Professional Football Researchers Association)
Steelers.com (Pittsburgh Steelers)

CHAPTER 10

Cfbhall.com (College Football Hall of Fame)
Lasportshall.com (Louisiana Sports Hall of Fame)
Profootballhof.com (Pro Football Hall of Fame)
Pro-football-reference.com (Pro Football Statistics)
Profootballresearchers.org (Professional Football Researchers Association)
Si.com (Sports Illustrated)

CHAPTER 11

Cfbhall.com (College Football Hall of Fame)
Donnieshell.com (Donnie Shell)
Ehbcsports.com (Black College Sports History and Legends)
Pro-football-reference.com (Pro Football Statistics)
Scfootballhof.org (South Carolina Football Hall of Fame)
Scstatealumni.org (South Carolina State University Alumni Association)

CHAPTER 12

Cleveland.com (City of Cleveland News)
Profootballhof.com (Pro Football Hall of Fame)
Pro-football-reference.com (Pro Football Statistics)
Steelers.com (Pittsburgh Steelers)

CHAPTER 13

Anaheimcolonists.com (Anaheim High School Alumni Association)
Cityofchampionssports.com (Pittsburgh Sports)
Grfx.cstv.com (University of Rhode Island Football History)
Jewage.org (Jewish Culture and History)
Kusports.com (University of Kansas Athletics)
Owlsports.com (Temple University Athletics)
Pro-football-reference.com (Pro Football Statistics)
Rockchalktalk.com (University of Kansas Sports)
Sports-reference.com (Sports Statistics)
Web.uri.edu (University of Rhode Island)

CHAPTER 14

Cfbhall.com (College Football Hall of Fame)
Profootballhof.com (Pro Football Hall of Fame)
Pro-football-reference.com (Pro Football Statistics)
Usctrojans.com (University of Southern California Athletics)

CHAPTER 15

Blackandgoldworld.blogspot.com (Pittsburgh Sports Blog)
Chicagonow.com (City of Chicago News)
Goleathernecks.com (Western Illinois University Athletics)
Nfl.com (National Football League)
Nolefan.org (Florida State University Sports)
Oklahomasportshalloffame.org (Oklahoma Sports Hall of Fame)
Okstate.com (Oklahoma State University Athletics)
Pasportshof.org (Pennsylvania Sports Hall of Fame)
Pro-football-reference.com (Pro Football Statistics)
Seminoles.com (Florida State University Athletics)
Theworldsstrongestman.com (The World's Strongest Man Competition)

CHAPTER 16

Cityofchampionssports.com (Pittsburgh Sports)
Jacksonville.com (Florida Times-Union)
Pro-football-reference.com (Pro Football Statistics)

CHAPTER 17

Calbears.com (University of California Athletics)
Cityofchampionssports.com (Pittsburgh Sports)
Pro-football-reference.com (Pro Football Statistics)

ABOUT THE AUTHOR

MERRILL SHAFFER is a lifelong (almost!) Pittsburgh Steelers fan, who grew up in Central Pennsylvania during the team's glory years in the 1970s. Like many dreamers, his football career did not progress much past those youthful backyard games and schoolboy days. However, his one football claim to fame was kicking off the first ball under the brand new lights during the first night game played at his high school football stadium. Realizing that a career with the Steelers may not be in the cards, Merrill earned an A.A. in Business Management from Harrisburg Area Community College and a B.S. in Criminal Justice from Pennsylvania State University. He has spent the past 16 years in law enforcement as a Probation Officer and remains a diehard fan of the Black and Gold. He is a member of Steelers Nation Unite and has had the pleasure of meeting and interacting with numerous current and former Pittsburgh Steelers players and coaches over the past three decades. Merrill resides in Palmyra, Pennsylvania with his wife and daughter.

Made in the USA
Monee, IL
18 October 2026

66035047R00059